Deep Calls to Deep

A Christian Spirituality of the Heart

Deep Calls to Deep

A Christian Spirituality of the Heart

by

George A. Maloney, S.J.

DIMENSION BOOKS
Denville, New Jersey

Published by Dimension Books, Inc.
Denville, New Jersey 07834

Dedication
To Josephine and Joe Santos and
to their beloved deceased son, Roberto,
who understand what *deep calls to deep* means.

Acknowledgments
Sincere gratitude to Sister Mary Faith, O.S.B., for her
generous efforts in typing this manuscript and for
proofreading the text and to Mrs. June Culver and Sister
Joseph Agnes for their suggestions, which proved most
helpful.

Imprimi Potest: Rev. Albert Thelen, S.J.
Provincial of the Wisconsin Province
of the Society of Jesus

ISBN 0-87193-286-5

Table of Contents

Introduction

God Trinity whispered in the silence of a muted, material world of beauty and multiplicity that God infinite wanted to be recognized and accepted by other creatures with whom he could share his very own life. "Let us make man in our own image, in the likeness of ourselves. . . . in the image of God he created him, male and female he created them" (Gn 1:26–27).

God dug deeply into the very inner core of his being, the triune community of Father, Son, and Holy Spirit and put into the hearts of the first man and woman and in all their progeny, you and me, their very own burning love for each other. But because we are created by God as finite, material human beings, God puts into us also a burning yearning, a deep down, aching pain, to know the triune family of God and to share intimately in their Spirit of love in a unity-of-difference.

We roam throughout this material world of ours, searching to discover more intimately the I-Thou-We of God's community in every flower we touch, in every sunset we cry out to with awe and reverence: "Oh, God!" Nothing, not even the oneness we experience in our human loves through the uniqueness of our two-ness and otherness, can ever take away this longing, aching pain within the depths of our being for greater oneness in the triuneness of God and for our uniqueness as a beautiful manifestation of God's presence on this earth in the incarnation of our "fleshness" with God's presence.

I look up at your heavens, made by your fingers,
at the moon and stars you set in place—
ah, what is man that you should spare a thought for him,
the son of man that you should care for him?
Yet you have made him little less than a god,
you have crowned him with glory and splendour. (Ps 8:3–5)

LIVING IN THE HEART

God has made us to live according to our true nature and to be at home, at oneness, with him. God's numinous or sacred presence was meant to be discovered within the inner depths of our being, called in Scripture our *heart,* as well as inside the material layers of the created world around us. We see the need to turn "within" in order to make contact with a sacred presence that is more powerful than we are. We long to know a sacred meaningfulness that will give ultimate direction to our lives beyond our immediate self-centered needs.

Yet in our exploding universe of today, the traditional views—as presented by Western Christianity, and based largely on an exhausted scholastic philosophy and theology that concern human beings, God, and the material cosmos—no longer seem adequate. A spiritual vision is needed to offset the Augustinian Platonism that has accounted for an unChristian separation of nature and supernature and a heavy dichotomizing between body and soul, matter and spirit, the secular and the sacred.

Our heavy rationalistic framework that has served to present Christianity to the West is in need of a complementary vision. Such a "new" vision is really not so new. It is found in the Old and New Testaments and in the ancient religions that discovered God immanently present in his created world.

Such *heart knowledge* is grounded more in perceptual, intuitive knowledge. It is an openness to God as mystery in which we meet the transcendent God in a reverential awe and wonderment. God's awesome transcendence cannot separate him from us. We are rooted in God as in our Ground of being. Yet that Ground is also rooted immanently within us. As Jesus Christ is the meeting of divinity and humanity with neither of them inseparable, and yet each of them distinct, so are we not to be separated, in all of our materiality and finite humanness, from God living within us, even though God is not man and man not God.

It is inwardly that we must go, into our hearts, that scriptural symbol of the interior "place" where we meet our Maker and Beloved in ever-expanding consciousness. This consciousness cannot be taught. It can only be evoked, awakened in the mind and heart by the transcendent power of God's Spirit. This consciousness of the divine presence, as loving, uncreated energies, abiding within us and without us, in each material atom of the universe, grows as we tune in more consistently to listen to God's revealing Word as he speaks to us in the cosmic signs of the material universe. His Word also speaks to us in our heart and reveals God's numinous presence in the signs of written Scripture as well as recorded history of the past and of the present moments in history now being lived and created with our cooperation. We can read these signs inside of us in the depths of our own consciousness and unconscious.

HEART SPEAKS TO HEART

As we learn to live more interiorly, our progress is a movement away from our masculine dominated, rationally controlled self to a more intuitive grasp of reality. A new knowledge is given to us: "heart knowledge." At first it is experienced as coming out of our deep reservoir where it seemingly always existed, yet was unknown to our superficial self.

Its depths seem to stretch downward into infinity. Gradually we have courage and sincerity to surrender to this new knowledge. We become aware that it flows from a communicating Person or Persons, indwelling within us. This Absolute Ground of our Being becomes gradually more and more present to us. We learn to let go and surrender to this loving presence. We experience an integrating process taking place between the feminine and masculine aspects within us. We are becoming an *I,* our true selves, now in free, loving dialogue with God as a *Thou*, an indwelling presence.

Integration takes place at this deep level, and it takes place most perfectly in the heart, that placeless place, where we can live fully on body, soul, and spirit levels through the Spirit's faith, hope, and love, in what we call *contemplation.* This is our human self standing, as it were, outside of our habitual ideas that we entertain of ourselves by getting down below that false everyday *ego* and touching in our deepest source the indwelling Trinity. Consciously and most freely we turn toward our Source and in the totality of our being, we humbly surrender in awe and wonder to the mystery of God's outpoured, personalized love in the Holy Spirit.

DEEP CALLS TO DEEP

I offer this book as my humble attempt to share with you what is the meaning of *heart,* its kind of knowledge as opposed to exclusive rational knowledge, and how we can in Jesus Christ encounter the heart of God and live in him through the pierced heart of Jesus Christ.

We, therefore, begin to look at the historical elements that account for the neglect of heart knowledge, chiefly in the Western world. Jesus in the Gospels calls us to the gift of heart knowledge by our becoming converted and becoming like a little child, filled with the gift of wonder. After a look at what mystical awareness or consciousness is, we investigate what heart means as a symbol down through the ages of all human cultures, but more precisely in the revealed Old and New Testaments.

As a condition of getting in touch with our heart we learn from the life of Jesus in the Gospels and the lives of all the great Christian mystics of East and West the absolute need of a *silent heart.* When we quiet our noisy minds and allow the Word of God to open up our heart, we discover much brokenness. As we learn to accept our brokenness deep within our heart consciousness, the Spirit of God and our spirit search for healing in God's triune love dwelling within us.

We learn from the early Christians how to pray in the heart by allowing the Spirit to pray with our spirit in wordless surrender to God's flaming heart. It is through the Word made flesh, Jesus Christ, dwelling within us as the risen Savior, that we discover how to enter into his heart, human and divine, and thus touch the deepest interior of God's perfect, self-emptying love for each of us individually, unto the last drop of water and blood.

We conclude the book by examining how in the heart of Christ we are driven forth by his Spirit to fashion ourselves into a synergism as co-creators with Christ through our cosmic heart. We see that only in a transformed heart living in unity with the heart of Christ can we also love all other human beings and all of God's material world, as we love ourselves. Such a *cosmic heart* is one with the pierced heart of Jesus Christ, as we go forth in his Spirit to empty ourselves for all human beings whom we meet and are privileged to serve. We strive to harmonize the entire world around us by the inner direction of the Holy Spirit and the Logos made flesh, Jesus Christ, to bring about the total Christ as we assist in the birthing of the universe into the cosmic Christ and help to reconcile the universe to the Father through his Son in his Spirit.

George A. Maloney, S.J.
Seal Beach, California
January 1992

1

Heart Failure

The French journalist Jean-Paul Kauffman was released by
Muslim terrorists in Lebanon in 1988 after three years of captivity. He described his relationship with God in his prison
confinement:

> I felt in that solitude that I had no one to speak to but God. I felt
> very close to him, then, perhaps because no one was there to
> distract me. I feel further removed from God now that I am back
> with my family in comfortable surroundings. In that prison, I
> was face-to-face with God. I almost miss the luxury of that soli-
> tude. I have a nostalgia for that intimacy with God. I try to find
> it now in my house in the country, but the intensity cannot be
> repeated.
>
> I knew that God was with me in my ordeal. I can't tell you
> how I knew, I just did. I felt that he would protect me. I avoided
> the opportunist trade of favors. I'll do this for you if you do that
> for me. I just said to him, "Let your will be done." . . .
>
> The problem with life today is that few people ever have to
> confront death. As a hostage, I was confronted with it daily, so
> fear wore off. . . . Suffering like that burns away all impurities,
> all that separates one from the honest contemplation of God and
> of oneself. I don't feel God in church, so I don't go. I have lost
> the intimacy with God. But I had it once. Once you experience
> God, you are forever changed.[1]

This journalist-hostage underwent great sufferings in solitude, and inner fears. Yet his basic fear of death was overcome by the experience he had of God as living in the deepest core of his being. This experience set him free from the exigencies of time and place. He was freed from the clamors of society and the opinions of others, dictating to him who he was as a doer, because he experienced his true *ego* in oneness with a loving, indwelling God.

LIVING IN A TRANCE

Technology has cast the human race into a trance. We walk about sleeping, unaware of an inner world of power, beauty, joyful play, and infinite love. Science has built a complete religion, based on the paradise myth of a material world of flowing oil and money, pontificated by the moguls of industry, attained by hard work on the part of all who wish to share in the kingdom of this earth. But we are being shocked out of our new religious torpor by the impending cataclysmic signs floating ominously in the West.

The Hindu poet Tagore, in the decade before World War II, voiced the problem which is still very much our own contemporary problem:

> Civilization is almost exclusively masculine, a civilization of power in which woman has been thrust aside in the shade. Therefore, it has lost its balance and is moving by hopping from war to war. Its motive forces are the forces of destruction and its ceremonials are carried through by an appalling number of human sacrifices. This one-sided civilization is crashing along a series of catastrophes at a tremendous speed because of its one-sidedness. And at last the time has arrived when woman must step in and impart her life rhythm to the reckless movement of power.[2]

Don Juan, in *Journey to Ixtlan,* teaches his disciple the necessity of "stopping the world." The disciple went into the desert and in silence listened to the real world for the first time. He saw what was always there, but most people fail to see. Don Juan explains:

> What stopped inside you yesterday was what people have been telling you the world is like. You see, people tell us from the time that we are born that the world is such and such and so and so, and naturally we have no choice but to see the world the way people have been telling us it is.[3]

THE JOURNEY WITHIN

We in the West are beginning to see the need of complementing "head" knowledge with another type of knowledge. We see the need to turn "within" in order to make contact with a sacred presence that is more powerful than we are. A sacred meaningfulness that gives ultimate direction beyond our immediate selfish needs is sought to offset the almost exclusive emphasis on rational knowledge.

We modern persons, heading into the twenty-first century, eagerly cry out to contact the *numinous* or sacred world, described by Rudolf Otto.[4] This cannot be taught. It can only be evoked, awakened in the "heart" by the transcendent power of God's Spirit. It is inward that we must go, into our hearts, that scriptural symbol of the interior locus or "place" where we meet our Maker and Beloved in ever-expanding consciousness.

This consciousness of the divine presence, as loving, uncreated energies abiding within us and without us, in each material atom of the universe, grows as we tune in more consistently to listen to God's revealing Word as he speaks to us in the cosmic signs of the material universe. His Word also speaks to us and reveals God's numinous presence in the signs of written Scripture as well as recorded history of the past and of the present moments in history now being lived and created with our human cooperation. We can read these signs also inside of us in the depths of our own consciousness and unconscious.

OUT OF THE DEPTHS OF OUR BEING

God has made us to live "naturally" at home in loving union with him. God's numinous or sacred presence was meant to be discovered within the inner depths of our being as well as inside the material layers of the world around us. We have always sought to look upon the face of God through myths and legends, symbols and sacred rituals. It is our technical world with its own religion of matter and the exclusive exaltation of rational knowledge over heart knowledge that has extinguished in our world the light whereby we can see God everywhere, live always in his loving presence, be joyful like happy children, be creative in developing the potentials that lie dormant that could bring forth so much creative love activity in our universe.

It is inside, into our hearts, that we must go. It is a terrifying journey that few of us have the courage to make. Many of us are attracted to the possibility of living constantly in loving communication and we make a valiant beginning. Most of us come running to surface after a short time. We miss the noise, multiplicity, the gaudy lights of the carnival and the raucous pitch of the hawker enticing us to see the greatest wonder on earth. The cotton candy and the sticky carnival apples delight us and make us forget what could have been.

PUTTING OFF THE JOURNEY

We possess the power for undoing ourselves and putting off the whole process of becoming healed of our fears and anxieties and meaninglessness and of being transformed into integrated persons, the ones that correspond to the name and person God knows us to be when from the depths of our being he calls us by our name (Is 43:1). We are masters at avoiding a confrontation with the real person that we could become if we could only put to death the "worldly" ego in us.

We have learned from earliest childhood how to play games, put up masks, become distracted by the words and values that people around us live by, expecting us also to follow their example. We can even busy ourselves "saying" prayers or, even in so-called "silent" prayer, refuse in real inner silence to look at our inner feelings, look at both the light and the darkness that are struggling to possess us.

As we indulge in such game-playing, it means we are afraid to be silent and meet God at the core of our being. We fear to look inwardly and honestly ask for healing from the transcendent God when we see through genuine self-knowledge what needs to be sacrificed, what needs to be transformed.

HEART FAILURE

Now that you and I are becoming older, is it not true that we catch ourselves reading with greater interest the obituary accounts in our newspapers? And how frequently we find that persons our own age, or even (gasp!) much younger than we are, have died of the most common cause of death: heart failure. We all know that when one's heart fails to beat anymore, the person is usually dead!

Yet there is in our Western world, even in Christianity of the West, a greater type of heart failure and cause of spiritual death than most of us are even aware of. And that is the failure of most of us to journey deeper into greater intimacy with the Trinity—Father, Son, and Holy Spirit—who dwell within what the Old and New Testaments call simply the *heart*.

This is evidently not our physical heart, but that placeless place within our deepest consciousness that is the seat of our human life, of all that touches us in the depths of our personality; all affections, passions, desires, knowledge, and thoughts, especially of beauty, joy, and love. It is in our "heart" that we meet God in an *I-Thou* relationship. The heart, therefore, in scriptural language, and as used by the early mystics of the church, is the center of our being, that which directs us in our ultimate values and choices.

It is the inner chamber where in secret the heavenly Father sees us through and through (Mt 6:6–7). It is where we attain inner honesty, integration of our body, soul, and the spirit relationships. In a word, where we develop "purity of heart" in order to see God everywhere (Mt 5:8).

PARADISE LOST

The first man and woman conceived by God in the garden of Eden are depicted in the book of *Genesis* as walking in his loving presence and communicating with him in the coolness of evening. "He put his own light in their hearts to show them the magnificence of his works. . . . Their eyes saw his glorious majesty and their ears heard the glory of his voice" (Sir 17:8, 11).

But man and woman lost the presence of God in their hearts. Instead of light, darkness and selfishness covered their innermost selves. They lost consciousness of their true identity and their loving relationships to God and to each other and to the material creation around them. They had been created with a hunger for God's beauty. They were made according to God's image and likeness, "male and female he created them" (Gn 1:27). And thus there remains the terrifying searching in every person for his/her true identity, for a loving relationship with God's communicating presence, his Word made flesh, Jesus Christ.

How can we understand this loss of heart knowledge, especially in our Western world, and in Western Christianity to a very great extent? Carl Jung lamented the fact that persons living in Western countries had become impoverished in their use of myths and symbols to transcend their horizontal optic in order to make contact with the Ultimate Ground of their being.

The technological power placed in human hands makes it difficult for us to experience a "creature-consciousness" before the awesome "Otherness" of God as the Ultimate Source of all being. We have also lost the presence of God within us, more intimate to ourselves than we ourselves are, to use St. Augustine's oft-quoted statement.

HISTORICAL REASONS
FOR LOSS OF HEART KNOWLEDGE

Because the symbol of heart referred to the affective sphere, it always had a leading role in poetry, literature, private prayer, and devotions in religion, in the Old and New Testament literature as well as the Christian liturgies. Dr. Dietrich Von Hildebrand insists that Aristotle's philosophy placed a ban on heart knowledge:

> According to Aristotle, the intellect and the will belong to the rational part of man; the affective realm and with it the heart belong to the irrational part in man, that is, to the area of experience which man allegedly shares with animals.[5]

Aristotle declared happiness to be the highest good for which we human beings seek all other goods. Yet he claimed knowledge to be our highest activity and disparaged the world of affectivity. But happiness becomes meaningless since it must be a "feeling" experience and not merely a thought of willed happiness.

St. Augustine, however, kept alive in the stress of Christian philosophy and spirituality the importance of heart affectivity that was embodied in the writers who followed Augustine's affective writing as Pascal, Duns Scotus, and the more biblically oriented mystics of the Christian East and West. But the majority of Christian philosophers followed Aristotle in giving to the human intellect and will the key to human superiority over animals, while the affections of the heart belonged to the irrational part of a human being, where one is most "animal." Such feelings had to come under the domination of intellect and will as an opposing enemy, had to be conquered and led into rational captivity.

LOSS OF AFFECTIVITY

Thus one's affectivity was associated with animal passions and was never a part of the spiritual life except in a negative way that such "feelings" and emotions had to be "mortified" or put to death. Much damage to an authentic Christian spirituality was done by reducing all affectivity to an impersonal state. Such a reduction deprived Christians of a personal experience of their own ultimate meaning and uniqueness. It removed affectivity from God's relationships with us, his children.

The intellect to know God's will through his commands and those of the church discipline and teachings, and the will to do his will, became the essential elements of the Christian life. This ruled out any true Christian affectivity to enter into such *I-Thou* relations between God and ourselves. God became more abstract, far away. He was seen by the majority of most Western Christians as an austere, punishing Judge toward his wayward, penitent children.

IRRATIONAL SENTIMENTALITY

The basis for true affective union between an individual Christian and God was ignored or equated with an irrational sentimentality. Joyful, passionate feelings in conjugal union were suspect and preached against as taking pleasures in irrational passions, while the primary end of marriage as procreation was exalted above any authentic feelings of mutual love. Liturgy was celebrated in Latin with its measured precision of expression and controlled reasoning. Little "feeling" was allowed to make such liturgical celebrations truly joyful events, as anticipation of the heavenly dance that awaits us in the life to come.

Mysticism was held in suspicion as dangerous and was brought under inquisitional condemnation as in the case of Meister Eckhart and so many women mystics of the Middle Ages, many of whom were branded unjustly as witches and burned at the stake for their visions. Contemplative nuns were put under obedience to a male cleric as spiritual director, who was to bring the right balance of intellect and will to rein in any wild hysteria of irrational affectivity.

As we are interested in this chapter merely to highlight the main causes for holding affectivity and heart experiences as anti-rational, we can postpone any discussion on proper or evil passions to later chapters. We should point out that throughout the history of Christianity there were authentic poets, philosophers, theologians, and mystics who kept a holistic balance between intellect, will, and heart in a holy synergism.

Blaise Pascal would defend such Christians who believed in heart knowledge, not in opposition to rational knowledge, but as a necessary complement. His statement: "The heart has its reasons which reason does not know."[6]

SPECULATIVE THEOLOGY

One main factor for repressing heart knowledge and the spirit of wonderment before the mystery of the living God in his loving activities toward his created order came through the separation of speculative theology in the twelfth and thirteenth centuries as Peter Abelard and Thomas Aquinas evolved a rational system of theology based on the rationality of Aristotle's philosophy with its disparagement of heart-affectivity. Theology was separated from *praxis* or the experiential and intimate union between God as Trinity and human persons and became a science of clear and distinct ideas. In fact, it was considered to be the Queen of all sciences! Faith would be described and lived as an intellectual assent given to a truth revealed by God through the teachings of the church. Lost was the body, soul, spirit, heart response on the part of the individual Christian.

St. Thomas Aquinas has done much to objectify God in his impersonalized, but not "real" relationships to us. He writes: "God's temporal relations to creatures are in him only because of our way of thinking of him; but the opposite relations to him are realities in creatures."[7] The weakness of our inherited Scholastic philosophy of the Middle Ages that colors Western Christianity lies in its inability to bring God into a scriptural, personalized relationship in temporality and in matter with us. God is seen as a "cosmic-do-gooder," content only to give us created things, but not to give himself in self-emptying love, bursting forth from the triune community of love, as revealed by Jesus Christ, the image of the Father and his Spirit of love.

It was Rene Descartes in the seventeenth century who believed that the key to understanding the universe lies in discovering its logical order., With Newton, Descartes thought of nature, including God, as "static" and obedient to basic, universal laws. "I think; therefore I am" was Descartes' contribution to the dichotomy he drew in seeing human beings as having two distinct and separable parts: a body and a soul or mind. We were more mind caught in a material body that would eventually die, but we would live forever because of our "immortal soul."

IN SEARCH OF MYSTERY

Edwin Scott Gausted, in his book *Dissent in American Religion,* points out that a great religious dissent is taking place in America, and it is moving in three new directions.

"Dissenters opt for mystery, seek community, and embrace joy."[8] He points out that Americans are more and more seeking mysticism over a clinical rationality. The theology handed them for so long has become for them remote and lifeless, and has been too much tied with an ecclesiasticism that has become impersonal and "correct," but does not speak to the needs of modern persons, nor flow out of experiencing the Word of God in Scripture.

On the positive side he points out that mysticism is awakening the powers of human creativity. A person who seeks mysticism is ready to be surprised by the hidden beauty that is in creation. Pointing out the low road that the quest for the mysticism of the heart can take, with all of its self-seeking, Gausted described the "high road" that the same quest can take:

> Deliberate acceptance of mysticism leads along the high road to humility. Man does not and will not know all, he cannot and need not control all. That high road also leads to the humane, to the needs of the person more than the dictates of the machine.[9]

Jesus clearly taught his disciples that we must be converted and take on the characteristics of little children:

> I tell you solemnly, unless you change and become like little children you will never enter the kingdom of heaven. And so, the one who makes himself as little as this little child is the greatest in the kingdom of heaven. (Mt 18:3–4)

Let us examine what a conversion to discover the *heart* within all of us means by seeing how to recapture the main characteristic of this spiritual childhood through developing the lost art of living in our hearts through the gift of *wonderment.*

2

The Gift of Wonderment

Dag Hammarskjold, the Secretary of the United Nations, writes in his beautiful work *Markings*:

> God does not die on the day when we cease to believe in a personal deity, but we die on the day when our lives cease to be illumined by the steady radiance, renewed daily, of a wonder, the source of which is beyond all reason.[1]

I believe that one of the most important gifts we need to rediscover in our Western technological world is the gift of *wonder*. Otherwise our lives become lives of hollow persons, as T. S. Eliot in 1925 prophetically described many of us who are living today:

> We are the hollow men
> We are the stuffed men
> Leaning together
> Headpiece filled with straw. Alas! . . .
>
> Shape without form, shade without color,
> Paralyzed form, gesture without motion.[2]

Our lives are filled with emptiness. We live in shades of black or gray. We suppress our native ability to understand the true meaning of God in our lives and to experience him as a loving Father. We cling to the prayer of petition where we see God as an object, a Santa Claus, to give us good things, and we never move into the state of continued praise and worship out of wonder for all God does out of love for us. We take for granted God, our loved ones (until they die), the very food and drink we enjoy in abundance daily, our freedoms in our country; but above all, we take for granted the miracle of our life when we lose the gift of *wonderment*.

Yet this is the malaise of all of us moderns coming from our almost exclusively national, scientific approach to life. Dr. Victor E. Frankl, the Austrian psychiatrist, confirms this sickness of almost universal meaninglessness that pervades modern society:

> Effectively an ever-increasing number of our clients today suffer from a feeling of interior emptiness which I have described as existential emptiness—a feeling of total absence of a meaning to existence.[3]

SCIENCE VERSUS THE WORLD OF WONDERMENT

Science creates the illusion that life is a bundle of problems that can all be solved by human reason. It begins with a curiosity, as does wonder, but it remains centered on the subject's power to observe, manipulate, control, and exploit the objective world outside. For such scientists, memory and the talk of childlike wonder are throwbacks to a childish and immature view of the real world. Since religion is connected with the invisible and mysterious world of an invisible God, reached by faith, hope, and love, religion is put down as an enemy to true science, the only entrance to reality.

In the scientific world all puzzles can be solved. There is no need to go beyond the visible world, governed by static and universal laws that always operate with absolute certainty; hence, there is no need for wonder.

Yet wonder does not oppose scientific, analytic knowledge, but is a most important form of a different knowledge that must supplement that of human reason. We find such knowledge exalted in Scripture. On every page of the Old and New Testaments, we see a radical amazement toward human history and nature due to an immanent God, all-powerful and all-wise, working in mysterious ways that lie beyond our reasoning comprehension, but are discovered by the humble and pure of heart.

There is found in Scripture the sense of perpetual surprise at the fact of our human existence, the existence of all creatures out of God's free creation of this amazing world: "This is Yahweh's doing and it is wonderful to see" (Ps 108:23). Wonder is different from the curiosity that is a prelude to scientific knowledge that disappears when causes are determined and phenomena adequately explained.

For the prophet, wonder is a form of thinking—a new knowledge beyond reasoning. It is an attitude that never ceases and is climaxed in worship. But would you not agree that in our modern world, as technology advances, the sense of wonder declines on all levels our human involvement, including our religious attitudes? We dry up and die psychologically and spiritually, not for want of information, but for want of wonder and humble appreciation for the real. Life without wonder is not worth living! We lack, not a will to believe, but to wonder!

THE WORLD OF WONDER

Wonder, or radical amazement, is the prerequisite for an authentically balanced human existence. We are being confronted at all times everywhere in our world around us with the mystery and grandeur of God, especially in our intimate relationships with other human beings. The way of faith leads us through acts of wonder and amazement to discover God at the heart of matter.

Meditate on God's wonders.
Can you tell how God controls them
    or how his clouds make the lightning flash?
Can you tell how he holds the clouds in balance:
    a miracle of consummate skill?
When your clothes are hot to your body
    and the earth lies still under the south wind,
can you help him to spread the vault of heaven,
or temper that mirror of cast metal? (Jb 37:14–17)

But wonder is first engendered into our hearts by the mystery of our sheer existence, the fact that we *are*. The Psalmist never tires of wondering at how marvelously God has created him.

It was you who created my inmost self,
and put me together in mother's womb;
for all these mysteries I thank you;
for the wonder of myself, for the wonder
    of your works. (Ps 139:13–14)

If we ignore the wonders by taking them for granted, there is no worship in our lives, no music, no dance, no surprises, no excitement in life—in a word, no love!

We train ourselves in wonder by exercising faith in the mystery of God's humble, but mighty and powerful love that is active in each detail of our daily lives. In all events we invoke God's name and presence, and learn to surrender to the mystery of his loving activity for us as we open up to his uncreated energies of divine love operating at each moment.

CHARACTERISTICS OF WONDER

I am sure you have had many moments when you went beyond your own rational understanding of what you were observing in a given experience and entered into this mysterious world of wonderment. Can a mother ever forget the wonder that flooded her as she held the mystery of life, her firstborn child, in her arms? How close God was to her in the wonder of the creative power to give new life out of the mother and father's mutual love that incarnates a new and eternal life of their child.

Sam Keen, in his book *Apology of Wonder,* gives us some of the characteristics of the objects that bring us into the state of wonder:

> *Contingency* means that in raw experience the object we apprehend in wonder comes to us without bearing in its own explanation. . . . wonder-events are happenings, revelatory occurrences which appear, as if by chance, bearing some new meaning (value, promise) which cannot be immediately integrated into a past pattern of understanding and explanation.[4]

Another characteristic other than contingency is that of *mystery.* Gabriel Marcel gives us the distinction between *problem* and *mystery.* In a problem situation (such as science) there is a subject and object relationship, an *I-it.* But in the mystery of wonder there is an *I-Thou* relationship. There is an openness to oneness in union and no longer a subject distancing him/herself from the object "over there." Birth in all its phases of conception, pregnancy, birth-giving and nurturing new life can be analyzed, yet the net result of a new living person is a product of wonderment that cannot be captured solely in scientific, objective, universal terms. The knower and the known form a living and personalistic relationship.

Another characteristic of wonder is that of *presence.* When you open up to the uniqueness of a rose (which you may have looked at many times before you distanced yourself as a subject looking at an object), to *really* look at it, you enter into the element of presence so essential in the gift of wonder. In wonder we are, as it were, grasped by the object that seemingly initiates the encounter.

As subject you are no longer the primary, aggressive actor. Reality is charged with a personalistic, conscious relationship between two creatures. To be present to the uniqueness of every creature—be it a plant, animal, or human being—is to open yourself to the other, no longer as a mere object, but now as almost the receptacle of another consciousness, at least of the participated beauty of the Creator in the unique creature.

WONDER IS ALWAYS A SURPRISE

For those who experience wonder, it is always a *surprise* that dramatically bursts upon us with a suddenness that produces in us amazement or astonishment. We cannot create wonder because we cannot create for ourselves something that will surprise us. We cannot control it since it is a gift we cannot actively bring about or manipulate. Such an experience, such as contemplating God's beauty in a special kaleidoscopic spangling in the west of a burst of ever-changing colors, reduces us, in its suddenness and gentle power, to lift us outside ourselves and our habitual, rational ways of perceiving the world around us, to a sense of silence. God's sacredness and holiness melt into each other as we move into awe and reverence before God's beauty and power in such a silent openness in adoration of the Divine Maker of all beauty.

An accompanying effect upon us is a mental or emotional sense of "dis-ease," of not being at ease, not being in control of the situation. Hopefully, all of us have experienced this emotion when we discovered a deep love that united us with another person. A new dimension of meaning was being revealed to us that challenged our habitual, rational control of a given situation. We ask new questions in such a dis-ease situation. New life is bursting all over the skies of our consciousness and unconsciousness, and we come alive with a new excitement in the presence of God as love. When we love one another, God's love is being perfected in us (1 Jn 4:12).

DEATH-RESURRECTION

Basically we all fear the unknown. Is this not why we plan our daily activities to keep the unexpected and unexplainable to a minimum? We prefer being an old wineskin, no longer able to stretch when the new wine is poured into us, and it ferments. Thus we seek to "domesticate" our world around us. We wish no strangeness, no challenges, no crosses, no trials, no risks! We all basically long for surprises, new loves, new experiences, new challenges, but we also fear letting go of the familiar and of our habitual control over the familiar.

In an event of wonder that fills us with delight and pleasure, there is always a pleasant surprise that presents us with a situation of dignity, new values. But in wonder we must abandon the aggressive self-control since we must allow others simply to be and ourselves to rejoice in their unique presence. We touch the inviolable strangeness but uniqueness in the other, and doing so, we touch God's wonderful, sacred presence as the self-emptying Gift of Love to us.

Thus we encounter the cross and the call to embrace a cognitive dying to our illusions that our full authenticity as a human being can continue to create our own worlds and persons and even God without a death. This is the way Jesus lived his earthly life. It tells us that, if we wish to have a part with him, we too much live according to this universal law implicit in the wonder-experience. If you wish to live an authentic, human life as a person, living fully unto God's glory, you must lose your former way of viewing the world exclusively from your own self-centeredness. But if you hold on to that optic and exclude wonder in your life, you will surely lose your life as an authentically and fully alive, unique person.

MOVING INTO CONTEMPLATION

When we surrender to the experience of wonder, there is always a movement into contemplation, away from the exclusive, rational mode of relating to God and neighbor. The characteristic of contemplation is basically a new openness through a disciplined silence of our rational powers to allow the "other" to speak, to reveal itself or themselves to us in all their uniqueness and inner beauty. With human beings and God there is an attentive listening to understand that person as a gift to us.

In contemplating the "other" we move into a receptive passivity that shows itself in the relinquishing of our own activity as the prime source of all reality. We open up in an active receptivity to the prime source of all reality. We open up in an active receptivity to the uniqueness of the other person. Contemplation seeks to go beyond the fixedness in the already-known to be relaxed in receiving with reverence from the other. Humility is demanded and a willingness to appreciate new riches that come to us in our emptiness of rational power to control outside objects.

Such a "passover" experience in wonder brings to us a sense of delight and enjoyment of new-found enrichment. The seed dies and brings forth a hundredfold. Out of amazement and admiration there grows gratitude for the gift being given to us. Such gratitude leads us toward celebration of our new-found richness, the new release of life and beauty. Toward God we move in worship as we enter the experience of his holiness as self-giving, as *Victim* and *Giver*. It calls us to celebrate in worship, not merely in words of praise, but in actual oblation of ourselves back to God as Victim and Giver in Christ Jesus. There can be no substantial difference between wonder and the experience of the holy.

BECOMING LIKE LITTLE CHILDREN

Jesus taught us in the Gospels the need for such wonder by calling us to a conversion to become like little children.

> I tell you solemnly, unless you change and become like little children, you will never enter the kingdom of heaven. And so, the one who makes himself as little as this little child is the greatest in the kingdom of heaven. (Mt 18:3–4)

Children have the ability to find sustained and continued delight in a state of marvel and amazement. The life of a healthy child manifests a freshness and anticipation and openness to the present moment that holds out the possibility of a child always being ready for a happy surprise. Sam Keen describes the world from a healthy child's viewpoint:

> The world is a surprise party, planned just for me, and my one vocation in life is to enjoy it to the fullest—such is the implicit creed of the wondering child. . . . To wonder is to live in the world of novelty rather than law, of delight rather than obligation, and of the present rather than the future.[5]

God's revelation of his reality in self-giving and his immanence to us at all times is the basis for our faith upon which we build the wonderment of a child at all times before its heavenly Father. Retaining this true filiation as a child of God, we are called also to be adults who can enjoy an even greater sense of wonder through the gift of the Holy Spirit. We can enjoy a greater openness to God's amazing humility and love in his creation of this universe, in the perfect gift of his incarnate Word Jesus Christ, indwelling us through his Holy Spirit.

When our wonder before the triune God becomes an habitual attitude giving us new eyes of faith, then we will understand that true wonder leads always to true worship of

God. Then the words of D. H. Lawrence will become a reality: "The sense of wonder, that is our sixth sense. And it is the natural religious sense." In a spirit, therefore, of wonder, let us seek to describe what is this *heart* we are speaking about. Let us remain like little children, not eager to define the human heart in rational terms clear to all thinking persons. Let us, rather, wonder at the mystery of the human heart that has its own reasons and logic not known to anybody but to converted children.

3

A Mystical Consciousness

Philosophers and science historians, such as Thomas Kuhn in his important book *The Structure of Scientific Revolutions,*[1] help us to talk about important shifts that through human history have taken place as one "paradigm" has supplanted an earlier and more outdated view to express human consciousness in relationship to the surrounding world. These paradigms allow us, first as individuals, then as whole cultures, to become liberated from the limits imposed by an earlier model of reality and to embrace a new and better model.[2]

Lewis Mumford describes such shifts in global consciousness:

> Every transformation of man . . . has rested on a new metaphysical and ideological base; or rather, upon deeper stirrings and intuitions whose rationalized expression takes the form of a new picture of the cosmos and the nature of man.[3]

But I would maintain that we do not need a new "system" or a new particular way of thinking about us human beings in relationship to the cosmos around us, nor do we need a new ideology. What is needed is an integrating *fourth dimensional consciousness* that will embrace all other levels of developed human consciousness. Yet it must raise also all other former levels of consciousness to a new and higher level. It must resist presenting merely another "rational" perspective that would lock us into our own human, limited, and even sinful thinking as we further a consciousness that is centered solely on human rationality as the exclusive source of all human knowledge.

A FOURTH DIMENSIONAL CONSCIOUSNESS

Such a fourth dimensional, integrating consciousness is new, and yet is it very ancient. It is the mystical, meta-rational awareness that all authentic mystics of all true religions have passed on in their small band of disciples. It can be called "heart knowledge." It is what all the Eastern Christian spiritual writers describe as the pushing of the mind down into the *heart*.

It is the global consciousness of all authentic mystics of all times of their oneness with all of created nature, with all other human beings as sisters and brothers of the one human family, with God as the Source of all their happiness and all ultimate meaningfulness. It is their interior prayer, prayer in the "heart," that such mystics of ancient and modern times have lived in human joyful contact and total surrendering obedience to God as they reached for the Promised Land through the inward journey into greater global consciousness of oneness with God, their Source, and with all other creatures.

Before I describe what in human history, especially in the Old and New Testament traditions, has been the meaning of *heart,* I would like to place such heart consciousness in its relationship to the other historical levels of consciousness development.

It is Dr. Jean Gebser who, in his contemporary work *The Ever-Present Origin,*[4] borrows the term the "fourth dimension," from Einstein, who used it to formulate his theory of relativity in 1905. Gebser uses it to refer to the mutation of human consciousness, that, like all previous mutations, is already present, latent in us, but bursts forth to become a consciousness of "world-building."[5]

FROM THE FIRST STAGE TO
RATIONAL CONSCIOUSNESS

Gebser gives us a convenient, historical outline of the development of the three stages of human consciousness that led to the formation of the first "axial period" in Dr. Karl Jaspers's term,[6] or the birth of human rationality that would evolve into our modern age of science.

1. The first stage Gebser calls *archaic consciousness*. The human being is characterized as experiencing him/herself as one with the universe without having any concept of space, time, or an individual *ego*. Primitive human being merged in identity with the created world around him/her.

2. *Magical Consciousness* followed. As in the former stage, a defined sense of an individual *ego* is still lacking, and there is a continued sense of fusion or union with all of nature. But what distinguishes this stage of consciousness is the decadence into which human beings fell as they yielded to degenerated forms of sorcery.

3. *Mythical Consciousness* was a turning point in giving human beings a sense of having an individual *ago* through an intellectual mind or soul. With intellectual awareness developed, human beings entertained a sense of the "otherness" of both themselves and of a Supreme Being. Still there was needed a refinement of mythical thinking.

4. *Mental Consciousness* is the turning point from mythic to self-reflective thinking. At this time the great religions were genuinely born and our fundamental categories of thought arose: in China with Confucius and Lao-tzu, in India with Gautama Buddha, in Persia with Zoroaster, in Greece with Thales, Pythagoras, Socrates, and Plato, and in Israel with the prophetic movement.

In the West this level of mental consciousness evolved through Plato's ideas and Aristotle's philosophy and science to separate all prior forms of consciousness from the one, exclusive form of rational consciousness. This fostered the rapid development of the objective science of deduction and induction, but prepared for the Cartesian world of the human mind as the essence of what it means to be human: "I think; therefore I am." The world of duality and of extreme dichotomy separated matter from spirit, God from his universe.

In the East such overrationalism was not attained since elements of prerational consciousness occupied an important part of mental awareness. It is in the context of the new movement in the West that we discover a mystical consciousness that will integrate the best of the stages of mental consciousness and the preceding ones into a holistic consciousness that will allow us to live in real, indefinable experiences of new living relationships of an *I* to the *Thou* of God, to other human persons and to an energized, personalized world.

CHARACTERISTICS OF THE
MYSTICAL CONSCIOUSNESS

In order to avoid viewing this fifth level of consciousness as an added level, we must outline the key characteristics of each mystical vision of reality.

1. We must see this fourth dimensional consciousness, not in opposition to any of the previous levels of human consciousness, but as an integrating force that takes the best from the previous levels, especially the three dimensional world of modern science, and raises those positive elements to a new and more sublime, open-ended, and holistic experience of God and all his creation.

2. We of the West see also the absolute need to offset the belief in the validity of rational thinking to the exclusion of any other mode of the more intuitive, "heart-felt" knowledge. Our technical rational world has presented nature as a self-

enclosed machine-like structure, set apart from both God and human beings, for the sake of domination and exploitation.

We can no longer live in relationship to our material world, to God, to ourselves, and to each other exclusively according to the classical framework that evolved in the Western world through Aristotle and Newton. Such a vision places the human being, the observer, as the center of all reality. Such a vision denies *holism,* the sense of the unity of all beings and the mutual belonging to each other through dependent, interacting relationships.

Albert Einstein strongly suggested that science and mysticism need not be enemies, but the rational needs the mystical:

> The fairest thing we can experience is the mysterious. It is the fundamental emotion which stands at the cradle of true art and true science. A knowledge of the existence of something we cannot penetrate, of the manifestation of the profoundest reasons and the most radiant beauty, which are only accessible to our reason in their most elementary forms—it is this knowledge and this emotion that constitute the truly religious attitude; in this sense, and in this alone, I am a deeply religious man.[7]

3. Related to breaking from the almost exclusive supremacy of human rationality is the need for Christians to push beyond the conceptual truths of Christianity to which most Christians have been content to give an intellectual assent, and to open such faithful to experiencing God and each other more immediately and directly in what Scripture calls our *heart.*

We do not deny the value of positive or *cataphatic* theology, but we need to experience God in an *apophatic* theology—directly, and in an experiential, intuitional knowledge. A person who experiences God in a knowing by "not-knowing" breaks through the seeming paradox, that the closer one comes to union with God, the more blinding God becomes to our own control and rational powers. This is not a matter of the knowledge of God becoming more abstruse, but of the divine nature itself becoming more present to those who in their brokenness call upon him to heal them of their ignorance and blindness. Those who purify their hearts shall truly see God through new spiritual eyes (Mt 5:8). The presence of God is brought about by the uncreated, dynamic, self-giving God in his creative, energetic love-activities taking place in and around us at all times in every event.

TO BE IS THE ANSWER

4. Our Western world is in great need of developing the power of simply "being," in contrast to always "doing." Yet how few of us have the inner discipline to be wrapt up in contemplating a simple scene of nature, a sunset or sunrise, the smile of a baby; to hold an acorn and already see the oak tree; to walk in the rain and be spiritually cleansed of all artificiality that separates us from the raw nature around us? Father Lassalle wisely points out that we have a need to be set free from "clock time."

Through development of mental consciousness, conceptual time or quantitative "clock time" came into being. Lassalle writes:

> Here for the first time a sharp delineation is made between past, present, and future. Time measures and divides. . . . This new form of time eventually cut the mythical view of the world into shreds.[8]

Mystical consciousness does not reject time, but gives us freedom from the slavery that holds us in bondage to doing things in time slots in order to have our identity. It frees us from the anxiety and worry of always running out of time.

5. Another important element of mystical consciousness is that of discovering the true essence of God, of ourselves, of all human beings, of all material nonhuman beings—by passing

through the limitations that we imposed by our deductive, rational powers to "uncover" by contemplation the true nature hidden within. Teilhard de Chardin taught Christians to discover Jesus Christ shining "diaphanously" throughout the entire material world.[9] Other writers speak of the transparency of the material creation that allows persons of contemplative power to go through the limitations of concepts and words to the inner essence of God and all of creation.

SEEING THE LOGOI IN THE LOGOS

It was St. Maximus the Confessor who developed the doctrine of a *Logos* mysticism of finding all of creation, each essence, in the creative Logos of God. This basis for true Christian contemplation is revealed in John's prologue:

In the beginning was the Word:
the word was with God
and the Word was God.
He was with God in the beginning.
Through him all things came to be,
not one thing had its being but through him. (Jn 1:1–2)

Sin caused the unity in God's universe to become splintered into antipodes of the created world versus the uncreated God, the sensible as opposed to the intelligible, the earth against heaven, the world opposed to paradise, masculine as opposite to feminine. We human beings stand between heaven and earth, possessing both spirit and matter. We must first discover within ourselves our unique *logos* in God's creative *Logos* and then perform our God-given task of mediation between the rest of the created cosmos and its Creator. For us Christians it is through the Logos-made-man that we can effect this unity, first within our own lives, then through our Christified, divinized natures, to creatively release the *logoi* of all creation in the cosmos.

The logos of each creature is its principle of harmony that shows us that relationship of a given creature to God's total order of creation and salvation. The whole world is interlocked and interrelated, but only we rational beings are capable of discovering the diaphanous, harmonious relationship between the *logoi* and the *Logos*.

In the seventh century, St. Maximus the Confessor wrote:

> Just as the sun when it rises and lights up the world manifests both itself and the things lit up by it, so the Sun of Justice, rising upon a pure mind, manifests itself and the essence of all the things that have been and will be brought to pass by it.[10]

Such knowledge supersedes any and all mere rational knowledge through deduction. It is a gratuitous gift that necessitates a slow but consistent death to self-love and attachment to worldly possessions. It sees beyond the appearances and unlocks the world to reveal to us the transparent harmony existing among all creatures. Such contemplatives are able to enter somewhat into God's very purpose, into God's very mind, to see the *raison d'être* of each created being and then to act lovingly according to that "logos."

A HOLISTIC SPIRITUALITY

6. The final key characteristic in a mystical consciousness is that of perceiving all of creation in its "at-oneness" in and through God's uncreated energies and interrelated to each other in the inter-harmony and ultimate unity of all things in God and God in all things. Our mental consciousness, especially through science, has brought about an anthropocentric vision of all reality. yet we see today the inadequacy of such a human-centered view of the cosmos.

The gigantic, almost apocalyptic extent of today's problems, especially in the pillaging of our natural resources, water, and air pollution, the increasing list of extinct or endangered species of birds and animals, the far-reaching effects of pesticides, the wanton dumping of industrial chemicals on land and sea, the overwhelming accumulation of waste, garbage, and junk, with the spread of poisonous toxins in the air, water, and through the earth, call out for another way of perceiving our human relationships to the world around us.

What is needed is our becoming rooted in God in a *theocentric* vision of the universe. In such a view as revealed by God in the mystical consciousness, all creatures are to be coordinated into a whole, into a dancing harmony. The world from God's viewpoint is one. All creatures, through the creative inventiveness and synergism of us human beings working with God, were meant to be interrelated in a harmonious wholeness. Each part has its proper place within the entire universe. Each creature depends on and gives support to all the others in one great body, all of which has been created in and through God's Word.

In such holistic spirituality the dualism between the material and the spiritual worlds is overcome. Body is not opposed as a part of a human person's makeup to the soul or the spirit. No longer is there the either/or dichotomy separating the profane world from the sacred. Such a vision of the unity and interdependence of all of nature can never be deduced from Euclidean axioms.

This is where the American Indian, the Hindu, and the Buddhist monks can teach us how to recapture the art of turning within and listening in order to go beyond the mere periphery of what we consider to be reality. Carl Jung has said that as Western people, if we are to save ourselves from further decadence, we must eventually develop our own Western form of yoga. By this he did not mean merely doing the *asanas,* Indian breathing exercises of sitting in the lotus position. He meant entering deeply within ourselves and hearing the true Self, the Absolute Ground of all being, tell us through experiential knowledge and enlightenment, that the world of senses is not the totality of reality, but that through an experience of our own unique oneness with the indwelling God we are really one with all being.

CONCLUSION

Now we are in a position to examine the mythopoetic symbol of heart. Examining the different levels of human consciousness has prepared us now to look at heart knowledge. In this way we will not insist, therefore, on an exclusive rational way to discover the complete essence of any given creature through analysis of our puny rational minds. With the wonderment of children, who are at home with the mysteries of myths, we can bring to our topic of heart knowledge a both/and approach and thus avoid an either/or dichotomy that would betray the best in poetry, art, music, dance, liturgy—and, above all, the best in true religion as essentially the entrance into the heart language to authentic love.

4

What Does Heart Mean?

This past Christmas I reread that childhood classic entitled, "Yes, Virginia, There Really Is a Santa Claus." It describes the world of childlike wonder and joy that come from faith, hope, and love of God's Spirit.

This world unfortunately becomes lost to most adults once they have become educated to believe that the only knowledge is that which is rational and logical, discursive and understood by our own intellectual powers. Any other knowledge is mere poetry, the fantasy of starry-eyed children before they stop believing in things like Santa Claus.

This little piece first appeared in the fall of 1897 as an answer given by an editorial writer of a New York city paper (now defunct) to the inquiry of a little girl named Virginia. She had written the editor of that paper to inquire whether Santa Claus really existed. The writer explained what would happen without experiences of the heart:

> There would be no childlike faith, then, no poetry, no romance to make tolerable this existence. We would have no enjoyment, except in the sense and sight. The eternal light with which childhood fills the world would be extinguished. . . .
>
> Did you ever see fairies dancing on the lawn? Of course not, but that's no proof that they are not there. Nobody can conceive or imagine all the wonder there are unseen and unseeable in the

world. The most real things in the world are those that neither children nor men and women can see. Only faith, fancy, poetry, love, romance, can push aside that curtain and view and picture the supernal beauty and glory beyond. Is it all real? Ah, Virginia, in all this world there is nothing else real and abiding.[1]

We are distinguished from other animals by our inexhaustible quest for happiness through self-knowledge, but also through affective experience of our union with God, the Supreme Source of all beauty, intelligence, but above all of love itself. We can rove over the earth, conquering oceans, mountains, and all conceivable natural forces. But eventually we must return to ourselves and enter within to search for the talisman that will unlock the hidden treasures of unending happiness. This inner case, or "guha" as the Hindus call the heart, is what all cultures have considered as the locus within all human beings where we can discover our unique, beautiful self in joyful union with the Source of all beauty: God himself.

THE MEANING OF HEART IN ANTIQUITY

That we might be able to enter into the mystery of heart knowledge of which Western culture is in such desperate need, let us begin to see what the ancients considered to be the heart. Our research will have to be limited, of course, but hopefully we will discover some predominant traits that commonly occur in most cultures when in history people of those cultures strove to describe the heart.

First of all, every human being is aware of his or her own physical heart, as were people of ancient cultures. The heart is a physical organ that pumps life-giving blood to the entire person; hence, it is universally taken as the symbol of life but also of inner strength and courage. We see this symbol carried out in a number of ancient societies that had the custom of eating the heart of one's enemy to acquire his strength.

In ancient Aztec culture, and earlier the Maya, the heart was considered to be the most precious part of the person and was offered in religious services to Tlaltecutli, the lord of the earth, by the removal of a living heart and by shedding of human blood.

Among the ancient Egyptians, the heart was not only the principal organ of physical life but was also conceived as the center of all human emotion, courage, and spiritual life. Thought, will, and wisdom reside in the heart. It becomes the locus of what constitutes a human being, a unique person capable of relating to the gods in prayer and love. Memory is stored somehow in the symbol of heart as it witnesses to the deeds of courage one has accomplished during life.

THE HEART IN FAR EASTERN RELIGIONS

In the *Upanishad* collection that formed a late part of the Hindu Vedic literature, we find not only the heart as the natural symbol of the center of life, but now all the inner faculties of the human psyche find their place in the heart. The heart is described in *Brhadaranyaka Upanishad* (3.20–25) as the place where everything that exists takes shape such as faith, supra-intellectual knowledge, ontological truth, speech, and all biological life.[2] Hinduism adds techniques of spiritual meditation that have as their goal the passing from the unreal and illusory to the real world of the gods. The heart is the place of divine vision and an entrance into transformative knowledge of union with the Absolute Source of all being through the *Atman* or Divine Breath within the contemplative.

To reach this bliss and union with *brahman*, vigorous asceticism must be practiced to purify the heart of all that clouds it from becoming "a polished mirror" to reflect the divinity that a human person always has within his/her heart.

The ancient Greek world had a much less subtle under-standing of heart where heart (*kardia*) for the Greeks becomes the place of the soul's life, the affections, emotions, and the feelings. Plato developed the theory of the tripartite soul. Above the diaphragm the mortal soul, the *thumos,* which inspires courageous deeds, exists. Below are the passions, and the immortal principle of the soul is in the head.

Aristotle would situate sensation, all sense knowledge, memory, and imagination in the heart, but the *nous,* or intelligence, is not attached to any physical organ.

HEART IN THE BIBLE

The Hebrew word for heart, *lev,* occurs over a thousand times in the Old Testament, which shows how important a role it played in Hebrew life and literature. The heart is the organ without which there would be no life, since all vital powers are concentrated there. It was both receptive and active, as the place not only of all psychological and intellectual life, but also of moral actions or conscience in relation to God's law.

It is in the heart that one understands divine things, and hence the heart is the place for centering, recollecting the presence of God, and remembering God's wondrous deeds to the people of God and to each individual person. The heart is one's interior or *qerev* upon which God implants his laws. "Deep within them I will plant my Law, writing it on their hearts" (Jer 31–33).

The heart, therefore, is the place where God actively implants his moral laws and empowers the individual to act righteously in keeping with his laws. It is the heart that is the center of one's religious relationships with God and neighbor. In the heart one learns to fear God and be obedient by acting faithfully according to the *hesed* covenant God has freely entered into with his chosen people.

> Yahweh, God of our ancestors, of Abraham, of Isaac, of Israel, watch over this for ever, shape the purpose of your people's

heart and direct their *hearts* to you. Give Solomon my son a heart determined to keep your commandments, your decrees, your statutes. (1 Cor 29:18–19)

During the Hellenistic age with the translation of the Old Testament books into Greek (the Septuagint version), heart took on a new meaning that resulted from the mingling of the Semitic and Hellenic meanings of the symbol. Thus heart, *kardia* in Greek, retained the Hebrew meaning of *lev,* but added Hellenic overtones so that heart became the place for thought and memory as well as for the religious life in obedience to God's holy will through his revealed laws.

HEART IN THE NEW TESTAMENT

The writers of the New Testament books effected a synthesis of both the Semitic and the Hellenic understanding of heart, but based on the belief that through Jesus Christ and the Holy Spirit the prophecies of the Old Testament were fulfilled in a new way. Yahweh had promised his people a new heart (Ex 11:19). The first Christians lived as with one heart and one soul (Acts 4:32). Jesus Risen and his heavenly Father came and dwelt in the hearts of the believers. Their very bodies were now temples of God since the Holy Spirit dwelt within them (1 Cor 3:16; 6:19).

Thus belief in Jesus Christ as the Son of God, who died for love of us human beings, whose blood poured out of a pierced heart on the cross, confirms the passionate love of God the Father for his people of the new and everlasting covenant as manifested through the humanity and his human heart. This reality was understood by a new knowledge of the heart given by the outpoured Holy Spirit. The heart, therefore, for Christians becomes now not only the physical symbol of human life including the emotional, intellectual, and volitional powers of the human person, but for the baptized Christians who have received the fullness of the Holy Spirit as dwelling in the heart, the heart becomes a metaphor to indicate the Christian's inner self, where the spiritual life is born and develops.

THE HEART AS BODY, SOUL, AND SPIRIT

St. Paul united the Greek concept of body and soul as forming the essence of the human being, yet he adds to the Semitic promise of the infusion into us human beings of the Spirit a new and essential element of what it means to be a fulfilled human person. "May the God of peace make you perfect and holy; and may you all be kept safe and blameless, *spirit, soul,* and *body,* for the coming of our Lord Jesus Christ" (1 Thes 5:23).

St. Irenaeus in the second century, the first great Christian theologian, built a theological anthropology upon the scriptural teaching of human beings made according to the image and likeness of God (Gn 1:26–27) and this text of Paul's from his first epistle to the Thessalonians. According to his teaching, we are naturally made up of the powers of the *body* and *soul,* which form the imageness in all of us. But we are not completely made according to the likeness of Christ, the perfect image of God, until by the power of the Holy Spirit we receive our human spirit relationship to God in the Spirit's regeneration of us into the Father's children by grace.[3]

Irenaeus wrote:

> But when the spirit here blended with the soul is united to God's handiwork (*plasma*), the man is rendered spiritual and perfect because of the outpouring of the Spirit, and this is he who was made in the image and likeness of God. But if the Spirit is wanting to the soul, he who is such is indeed of an animal nature, and, being left carnal, shall be an imperfect being, possessing indeed the image of God in his formation, but not receiving the similitude or likeness through the Spirit, and thus is being im-

perfect. . . . Those then are the perfect who have had the Spirit God remaining in them, and have preserved their souls and bodies blameless, holding fast the faith of God, that is, that faith which is directed toward God and maintaining righteous dealings with respect to their neighbors.[4]

TO TOUCH GOD IN THE DEPTHS OF THE HEART

Jesus said in the Gospels: "What, then, will a man gain if he wins the whole world and ruins his life?" (Mt 16:26).[5] This means more that to lose one's earthly life. It means to lose that specific, secret center of our personality where all our values and eternal life, our oneness with the indwelling Trinity of Father, Son, and Spirit lie.

To find our eternal life means to find our real *I* by entering into the depths of our heart. It requires a new, spiritual birth, an awakening from the dead or a healing from our blindness. Only a religious, spiritual person who wishes to discover his/her unique depths, by a conversion in the heart, can reach this knowledge of his/her true self in Christ Jesus.

It is in the depths of our hearts that we can really touch God in a genuine religious experience. The Gospel incessantly affirms that the heart is the organ to receive the Divine Word as the earth receives the seed that produces great fruit as we cooperate with the transforming working of the Holy Spirit.

In the depths of the human heart under the power of the Spirit, we can touch God and have "heart knowledge" of absolute certitude that we are really children of God. Paul wrote: "The Spirit himself and our spirit bear united witness that we are children of God" (Rom 8:15). Here is where the dignity of being called by God to be made according to the image and likeness of Jesus Christ is realized, and through the Spirit we are divinized progressively more and more as we are made in our hearts "participators" of God's very own nature (2 Pt 1:4).

DEEP CALLS OUT TO DEEP

Until we human beings meet God in the depths of our being, in the heart that embraces not only the consciousness but even the unconscious, we will never understand the infinite love of God for us that, when experienced by us as immanently personalized in the self-giving Love of the Father, Son, and Holy Spirit within us, transforms us into our true selves. We will also never come into an actual and effective knowledge of our own inner beauty and uniqueness to be his manifestation of beauty and love in a way that no one else except our unique self can bring forth now in time and place and forever in the life to come.

Paul wrote of this type of heart knowledge that is gift from God, yet that transforms us to be filled with God's perfect goodness:

> Out of his infinite glory, may he give you the power through his Spirit for your hidden self to grow strong, so that Christ may live in your *hearts* through faith, and then, planted in love and built on love, you will with all the saints have strength to grasp the breadth and the length, the height and the depth; until, knowing the love of Christ, which is beyond all knowledge, you are filled with the utter fullness of God. (Eph 3:16–19)

DIVINE IMMANENCE

Christianity added a revolutionary element of divine immanence within us human beings that could never have been dreamt of by those of the nonChristian religions. This was not to be an assimilation whereby we would lose our identity as human beings. Rather, we would experience our true identity in loving submission to the triadic uncreated energies of God abiding within us. Jesus Christ teaches that, as a result of living in the heart according to the Word of God, we have a new immanent relation to the indwelling triune God. "If anyone love me, he will keep my word and my Father will love him and we will come to him and make our abode with him" (Jn 14:23).

Christian prayer allows us, by the Holy Spirit's gift of faith, hope, and love, to enter into a continued living experience of being "begotten" in our hearts by the Father in the Word through the Holy Spirit. Thus Christianity, as it evolved in the East, would mingle in a healthy synthesis the two basic polarities of God without and God within. The synthesis between a positive, rational understanding of God and a mystical, heart knowledge that best characterizes Eastern Christian spirituality has been called *hesychasm.* [6]

TRANQUILLITY OF THE HEART

Hesychasm was the form of Eastern Christian spirituality that revolved around the symbol of the heart. Hesychasm comes from the Greek word *hesychia*, which means tranquillity, peace, or integration. *Hesychia* is that state in which the Christian through grace and one's own intense asceticism, reintegrates his/her whole being into a single person that is then placed completely under the direct influence of the Trinity dwelling within the Christian. This formed the basic foundation for the spirituality of the men and women who fled into the physical deserts of Egypt, Mesopotamia, and Syria in the fourth century to "push their minds into their hearts" as they stood mindful of all the movements within their hearts, which embraced all body, soul, and spirit levels of thought, word, and deed.

As we have already pointed out from the New Testament understanding of heart, such athletes of the desert also saw the heart as that which symbolizes our transcendence beyond the world, the inner stretching power within our spirit to go toward God in thought and loving deed. It is the living out of God's command to love him with our whole heart, mind, soul, and strength (Dt 6:6). They took seriously the words of Yahweh expressed through the prophet Jeremiah: "When you seek me you shall find me, when you seek me with all your heart" (Jer 29:13).

The writers of Scripture were using a powerful symbol as a point from which, while still rooted in this world, the heart could swing free, moving into the fullness for which it was created, namely, to embrace God in the loving relationship of child to Father. The Fathers of the desert were only being scriptural when they used the heart as the place where we encounter God with all our strengths, but also with all our brokenness and sinfulness that cry out for healing from God. In their thinking, heart referred also to the "new creation" or, in Pauline terms, "the new man" that was healed, integrated, and transformed into a new creature in Christ Jesus (2 Cor 5:17).

HEART SPIRITUALITY

Pseudo-Macarius, who wrote his *Fifty Spiritual Homilies* in the latter part of the fourth century,[7] is one of the main influences in developing a Christian heart spirituality. He continues the Semitic influence with its accent on the total, existential encounter with God in the "heart," found chiefly in the Antiochene school of St. Ignatius of Antioch, Polycarp, Irenaeus, and Antony of the Desert.

God is encountered as the ground of one's being, primarily in the heart and not in the intellect or mind. Macarius insists on the total encountering in ever-increasing awareness and even "feeling" of that presence of the indwelling Trinity on body, soul, and spirit levels. The divinizing effects of the Holy Spirit work through grace to lead the Christian into ever-mounting levels of transcendent possibility, and realized human development according to the image and likeness that is Jesus Christ. Pseudo-Macarius described the function of the heart:

God's very grace writes in their hearts the laws of the Spirit. They, therefore, should not put all their trusting hope solely in the scriptures written in ink. For, indeed, divine grace writes on the "tables of the heart" (1 Cor 3:3) the laws of the Spirit and the heavenly mysteries. For the heart directs and governs all the other organs of the body, And when grace pastures the heart, it rules over all the members and the thoughts. For there in the heart the mind abides as well as all the thoughts of the soul and all its hopes. This is how grace penetrates all parts of the body.[8]

St. Theophan the Recluse (1815–1894), one of the outstanding nineteenth-century Russian mystics, described the heart in the Macarian hesychastic tradition:

The heart is the innermost man or spirit. Here are located self-awareness, the conscience, the idea of God and of one's complete dependence on him, and all the eternal treasures of the spiritual life. . . . Where is the heart? Where sadness, joy, anger, and other emotions are felt, here is the heart. Stand there with attention. . . . Stand in the heart, with the faith that God is also there, but how he is there do not speculate. Pray and entreat that in due time love for God may stir within you by his grace.[9]

THE HEART: CENTER OF ALL HUMAN LIFE

The heart, therefore, cannot be conceived as merely another part of our human makeup. The heart is the hidden, deepest consciousness within us as the religious organ whereby we can encounter the triune God as the true center of our entire human life, on body, soul, and spirit levels. The heart must be distinguished from the body, the soul with its emotions, imagination, intellect, memory and will powers and even from spirit level. Heart goes beyond even consciousness to embrace also the unconscious. It transcends all the powers of the body, soul, and even spirit levels of our human existence, and yet permeates all of them as the potential integrating "place" where grace and free will operate to bring about an integrated human person, totally submissive out of feeling love to the indwelling Spirit of God's love.

Thus we see that the outstanding and proper characteristic of Eastern Christianity, so rooted in Scripture and the experience of the early mystics of the church, lies in this—namely, that the mind with its intellectual reasoning powers, is not the ultimate foundation or core of our human life. An intellectual grasp of God through an intellectual assent to the reality of God based on Scripture is not the essence of true Christian religion.

Our Western civilization comes to us from the Renaissance, which sought to deprive the heart of its central position in the Christian religion. It highlighted the power of the mind, of science and consciousness while excluding by and large the central role of the heart. Yet it is in the heart that we discover harmony and integration of all other human levels of life, body, soul, and spirit. St. Paul summarizes the role of the heart and God's grace in giving us a knowledge beyond rational knowledge: "and that peace of God, which is so much greater than we can understand, will guard your hearts and your thoughts, in Christ Jesus" (Phil 4:1).

Therefore, we can summarize in general the meaning of *heart*. Every verbal definition or description must limp and fail to convey the full meaning of heart. As we have pointed out, heart is a placeless place, where at the core or center of our being, we discover the transcendence that makes us sharers in the very image and likeness of God. It calls us to stretch out in prayer to touch infinity in the life of the Trinity dwelling within us. It is permeated by God's active grace to draw us into greater oneness with the divine indwelling Trinity and give us our true, beautiful, unique self in our oneness with the risen Lord Jesus.

THE HEART OF THE NOT-YET

Yet both Scripture and the early Fathers of the desert and mystics down through the ages have described the heart as the "container" of the unconscious, the not-yet material that lies deeply in our roots that link us back, not only through our genetic preprogramming to the first man and woman of the human race, but to the material world from the first "big bang." Jesus himself taught us that out of the heart flow evil thoughts, evil powers that can destroy the divine life living also in the heart. "For from the heart come evil intentions: murder, adultery, fornication, theft, perjury, slander. These are the things that make a man unclean" (Mt 15:19–20).

Pseudo-Macarius described the heart as a mansion with many rooms:

> For all of us appear to be as one, both those who are with Christ and his angels and those who are with Satan and his unclean spirits. There are, therefore, infinite depths to the human heart. There are found reception rooms, bedrooms, doors and ante-chambers, many offices and exits. There is found the office of justice and of injustice. There is death and there is life. There takes place upright business as well as the contrary.[10]

A BROKEN HEART

The heart is the place of conversion, of healing and integration from our worldly ego or false self into our true self in vital, conscious relationship at all times with Jesus Christ through the Holy Spirit's gifts of faith, hope, and love. It is a place to confront the inner demons that rise up as a hostile army within us. It is in the heart that the necessary conversion to Christ as the Divine Physician takes place and the inner healing of our brokenness.

The ancient Greeks referred to the *daemon* or *daimon* within all of us. This refers both to the light and the darkness, the already saved and integrated, and the not yet within us. We have both positive and negative elements stored up in giant proportions to be actualized in creative or destructive thoughts, words, and deeds. We all veer dizzily, now toward sadness, at times, then toward noble love or back to cruel selfishness.

The *daimonic* in all of us can be unto good or evil; often it is a bit of both. It is never totally oriented toward beauty and creativity. We possess much brokenness within ourselves. But in that very brokenness lies unsuspected richness in new love energy.

We find a oneness with the whole world in our brokenness, in "the sin of the world." We find our darkness to be a part of the world's darkness. We have inherited it simply by being a part of the human race. But you and I are individual persons who have become what we are and what we will be through our actions upon and reactions to other individual persons. Our parents, friends, teachers, wife, husband, children, enemies, and even "indifferent" acquaintances have helped to make us what we are by their attitudes, act, and even, omissions. It is here in the so-called heart that we come face to face with the daimonic in us, that which is part of our broken state of inauthenticity. This also explains the good and the creative in our lives with its great potential for even greater beauty in the future.

COURAGE TO ENTER THE DARKNESS

It takes much courage to go deeper into our hearts and there to confront the dark side. For most of us, however, we fear encountering so much ugliness in forms of darkness and distortion, and so we learn tricks whereby we put off the true conversion of the heart. We will deal with this necessary area in another chapter as we encounter the *daimones* deep within our hearts. Suffice it to insist here that whatever the skein of knotted, twisted threads that have fashioned the tapestry of our lives (and so many of such influences have been beyond our control), there lies deep within us another self, that *true self* of unrealized potentiality.

In confronting our brokenness, we are driven into our creaturely nothingness. What can we do to extricate ourselves from these overpowering forces that have mostly come originally from without, but now lie like unchained, wild dogs within us? Such a confrontation with our inner brokenness and nothingness before such overwhelming forces of negativity and destruction can be the turning point to a new life, a life of crying out for God's mercy and healing love from the depths of our heart.

Deep within us lies the *real self,* the person unrealized as yet, but loved infinitely by the triune God. God's Spirit hovers over this chaos, the darkness that could blaze forth into creative light, peace, and joy if we would only stretch out and follow that thin, silvery streak of godly light out of the binding slavery into true freedom. It is here in our true self that God dwells, making his mansion (Jn 14:23) within us, as we become more and more spirit, communicating freely in intimate loving communion by God's Spirit with the indwelling heavenly Father and Jesus Christ.

Years of sorrow and repentance, tears of fright at our own non-being pour forth gently as God's soft, healing dew falls upon the cracked, parched earth of our heart to stir those seeds of new life into reality. Let us conclude this chapter and prepare for the following ones by learning through the following prayer-exercise to follow our breath into our heart.

PRAYER-EXERCISE

Prelude: In the Book of Genesis we read the important statement: "Then Yahweh breathed into his nostrils a breath of life, and thus man became a living being" (Gn 2:7). In the continued gift of breathing God's breath into our bodies, we have the possibility of coming to an inner awareness that should be the experienced reality that God is the Source of our very life. We breathe in God's living breath so that we can become partakers of his very own nature (2 (Pt 1:4).

In this simple but most important exercise we wish to learn how to become consciously aware, not by our own thinking, but by the experience within our heart, in our "entrails," at the center of our being, that God is our loving Giver of Life. The inhalation and exhalation of God in our breath is the primordial rhythm of God's uncreated energies of divine love within us and outside of ourselves.

In three stages of "right" breathing we will experience that, as we breathe, so we relate to God and the world around us. In the *first stage,* we become conscious of what has been taking place without our awareness, namely, of our usual physical breathing, of our usual pattern of breathing upward, toward the chest. We will then seek to bring our breathing downward toward the center of our gravity in a continued process of *letting go.*

The *second stage* consists in recognizing the faulty breathing along with the faulty perspective that directs such incorrect breathing: our refusal to let go of the narcissistic self. Our breathing patterns are concentrated on the upper, rational level, where our false selves are in power. We must learn in this second stage how to correct this by letting go. By trusting in God as the Source and Goal of all our inspiration and aspiration, we receive a new way of being.

In the *third stage* we begin the infusion of the Holy Spirit, not to think or imagine nor to seek to understand this new life, but by the Spirit's gift we see such deep breathing in the "heart" as a gift of new and eternal life and to surrender to that all encompassing life.

BREATH-MEDITATION

1. *Body Relaxation.* Choose a quiet place. Sit in a relaxed position on a straight chair and keep your spinal cord straight without bending or slouching. Close your eyes and begin to breathe consciously, slowly. . . . Relax each member of your body as you surrender to the living presence of God within you. Start releasing any physical tension as you concentrate first on your forehead, your face, throat. . . . Concentrate on your shoulders and relax them . . . on your arms, elbows, forearms, wrists, fingers. . . . Feel your fingers becoming heavy as your relax.

Move to your heart and lung areas, your abdomen, the genital area. Let go of any tension. Go down your legs, hips, thighs, knees, calves, ankles, and toes. You are becoming totally relaxed.

2. *Psychic Relaxation.* Try bringing your mind into a simplicity by transcending the multiplicity of thoughts, images, feelings, ideas, even moods that rise up spontaneously as you become more quiet. You transcend by "going down" into your heart, by gently letting go as you become still-pointed to the presence of the calming Lord Jesus.

3. *Spirit Relaxation.* As an enspirited being in oneness with God's Spirit of Love who resides within your heart, seek to feel your oneness as you surrender to the indwelling Trinity.

4. Now, relaxed into a wholeness of your being, begin this exercise of deep breathing:

With eyes closed, follow your breathing inwardly. Synchronize your inhalation with the opposing movement of the diaphragm muscle in your abdominal cavity. As you breathe in, this diaphragm moves outward. Do not breathe up in your chest area, filling only your lungs, but feel the double movement as one, natural movement.

See whether your normal breathing has been upward and not downward.

In the second stage, recognize your wrong breathing that indicates holding yourself "upward" in control, making yourself the center of all your activities. Learn to lose yourself in order to find your true self. As you open up in your breathing, open yourself to accept the new, and close yourself in surrender of the old. A trustful spirit of self-surrender to God as the true Source and Goal of all your striving opens you to a new confidence in a new and richer life in him as you discover the peaceful exhilaration of coming into your true self in him as the center of your breathing and your life.

In the third stage, as you yield to the cosmic movement of the divine ebb and flow from outside to the depths of your being in your heart, you experience the silent pulse of God's inspiration and respiration, and you surrender to your oneness in his eternal rhythm.

Continue to breathe diaphragmaticly and deeply. As you breathe in, learn to hold your breath for a fraction of a second, and then slowly breathe out as you allow the diaphragm muscle to move toward your spinal cord. You have reached the center of your gravity, and there you are living in the new life of your true being in oneness with the absolute Being. Yet you are also becoming aware of your beautiful, unique self as you allow God's uncreated energies of love to penetrate deeply into every cell of your being. God is love and life! You are becoming whole, unique, and beautiful as God's manifestation of beauty in human form on this earth to the degree that you immerse yourself in the gentle embrace of God as he cradles you into great being.[11]

5

The Silent Heart

Christianity is a religion built upon a desert spirituality. The historical exodus of the Israelites—from their slavery in Egypt, through a forty-year period of purification in the Sinai Desert, to their eventual entrance into the Promised Land—has become an archetype for all Christians. We, too, have been called by God from slavery to sin into our own inner desert, that of the *heart*. There we are to come into different levels of conversion, measured by the degree of freedom and affective will to surrender to the purifying love and guidance of our heavenly Father throughout all our earthly pilgrimage.

How easily we see ourselves in the stubbornness of the Israelites and their grumbling against God. We, too, cry out for living water and meat to eat (Ex 16:21). We, too, often yearn for a return to our unforgotten, if shameful, past of slavery and confinement and ask: "Should we not do better to go back to Egypt? . . . Let us appoint a leader and go back to Egypt" (Nm 14:4).

God never forsakes his people. The only question for us is this: How deeply into the desert of our own hearts do we wish to enter and there learn—by trial and tribulation—by purification and testing—how to surrender to the supremacy of his love? Jesus, also, was led into the desert of his heart by the

Holy Spirit (Mk 1:12), where he was given the choice between the isolation of self-centered concerns and the true solitude of surrendering in love to the Father's providential care.

The desert experience was for Jesus a daily struggle in his heart between the power and plan of his heavenly Father, and the lure and empty promises of evil. Often during his public life, following some thirty years of relative solitude in Nazareth, Jesus would retire into the desert, or other barren, quiet places, where he could be alone with the Father. He needed "connected aloneness" and "space" in his heart to experience his true self in his encounter with his loving Father as the Center of his being.

We are desert pilgrims also, because we are followers of those early Christians who learned to enter into the desert of their hearts and, by their faith, hope, and love, consciously welcome the risen Lord who alone could conquer all the sin and evil in their lives. The desert Christians of the fourth century, following the example of the Israelites and of Jesus himself, were even led by the Spirit into the physical desert where they could be reminded of the inner desert places within their hearts.

There they remained in silence and solitude, advancing to new levels of oneness with Christ and with the entire world as they came in touch with him, the Center of all reality, in whom God creates all things. Jesus often preached to his followers, including us in the twentieth century, that, if we wanted to have a part of him, we would have to deny ourselves, take up our cross each day, and follow in his footsteps.

This following will inevitably take us into the inner desert of our hearts where the forces of light and darkness constantly battle. But of the aridity and emptiness of that desert God brings forth something new. He re-creates us in the image of his divine Son, sharing with us his own divine life: "And for anyone who is in Christ, there is a new creation; the old creation has gone, and now the new one is here" (2 Cor 5:17).

NEED FOR WITHDRAWAL

Whoever aspires to attain this most intimate union with God must imitate the Israelites who fled from the Egyptians into the desert where they met God as their only Source of being and happiness. Among the early hermits of the desert, as St. Antony taught, such physical removal from the many temptations and cares of the world was considered the first condition to attain purity of heart.

Exterior and interior silence, in the words of St. Basil, is the beginning of purity of heart. Withdrawal from the things of this world would make no sense unless there was an inner withdrawal from attachments to persons, places, and things that impede a total attachment solely to the indwelling God.

INNER SILENCE

Today several theologians, such as Bernard Lonergan, are writing about the different stages of "conversion." Lonergan writes:

> Fundamental in religious living is conversion. When conversion is viewed as an ongoing process, at once personal, communal, and historical, it coincides with living religion. For religion is conversion in its preparation, in its occurrence, in its development, in its consequents, and also alas in its incompleteness, its failures, its breakdowns, its disintegration.
>
> Now theology, and especially the empirical theology of today, is reflection on religion. It follows that theology will be reflection on conversion.[1]

Such theological reflection on the different levels of conversion must be concerned with an individual's seeking God in his/her life and in relationships with others in active ministry. Such an understanding brings us close to the biblical sense of conversion as an ongoing process of moving through deepening faith, hope, and love to new, inner vision, a transformation out of the slavery to self-centeredness to the freedom of being children of God. It takes place on all levels of body, soul, and spirit relationships of one's daily life experiences.

Thomas Merton describes well such a renewed sense of conversion that was at the basis of the beginnings of monasticism as a living out of the scriptural sense of conversion:

> The Christian is . . . one who abandons an incomplete and imperfect concept of life for a life that is integral, unified, and structurally perfect. Yet his entrance into such a life is not the end of a journey, but only a beginning. A long journey must follow: an anguished and sometimes perilous exploration.[2]

Let us examine the important elements of inner silence and solitude that are the necessary concomitants to a true conversion on any and all levels. These two are the very breath that gives life to any inner conversion that transforms our human life from the worldly ego to one's true self in Christ Jesus. In a word, there would be no authentic conversion possible without inner silence and solitude.

There can be no true growth in deeper prayer and union with God without silence on all levels of our being: physical, psychic, and spiritual. Silence, especially on the spiritual level, becomes the inner poverty of spirit that Jesus calls blessed, for to such the Kingdom of God is given (Mt 5:3), and is experienced in what Scripture and all Christian mystics down through the centuries have called the *heart*.

Karl Rahner describes what happens when we enter into authentic silence:

> If we are silent, if we forgive, if without reward we give ourselves wholeheartedly and are detached from ourselves, we are reaching out into a limitlessness which exceeds any assignable bound and which is nameless. We are reaching out towards the

holy mystery which pervades and is the ground of our life. We are dealing with God.[3]

THE SILENCE OF GOD

To understand the silence of our heart as the foundation for conversion, we need first to understand the silence that exists within the loving community of the triune God, between the Father and his Word through the self-emptying love, the Holy Spirit. God is love, and silence is the perfect communication of the Father and Son through the Holy Spirit. Love needs no language, but it does express itself in perfect silence: the silence of surrendering love.

God needs no multiplicity and variety to express his eternal continuity in love. He loves through his one Word. His silence is not broken by speaking his Word. His Word issues forth eternally in silence. We need to punctuate our words with pauses in silence because we need to reflect, search out further ideals, correct or amplify what has just been said. God, however, speaks continually his unchanging Word. He never needs to utter a second or a third because in his Word he expresses perfectly all that he is since he expresses his Word through the loving, silent sigh of Love—the Spirit.

Speaking his Word in eternal silence through his outpouring Love, the Holy Spirit, the Father hears his Word come back to him in a perfect, eternal "Yes" of total, surrendering Love, again the Holy Spirit. The Spirit is the deepest expression of love uttered in ecstatic silence! Love pours itself out in silence of one Word uttered. But Divine Love is also the silence of repose in which the Word freely comes back to rest in the eternal embrace of his Father. "He who sent me is with me and has not left me to myself, for I always do what pleases him" (Jn 8:29).

But when God's creative energy fashions us human beings as his masterpiece of all material creation, he turns within and the *I* of God speaks to us within and in that loving silence says: "Let us make man in our own image, in the likeness of ourselves" (Gn 1:26). Of all God's material creatures we human beings are the only ones capable of hearing God's Word uttered in flaming Love, the Spirit, who invites us to respond to his very own nature (2 Ps 1:4). Only in prayer can we become aware of being personally loved by God Trinity. Only in prayer can we alone return that love—as in a godly silence, we still our own desires, plans, ideas of God, ourselves, and the world we constantly create according to our own inner noisy desires.

RETURNING TO OUR TRUE SELVES WITHIN

We need to turn within our heart and in silence we must enter deeply into our true selves and hear God's Word, Jesus Christ, the risen Lord, dwelling in oneness with the Father and Spirit, speak our name. This can only be discovered through the Holy Spirit in all our unique personhood as God's unique word in his Word, manifesting in human, material existence in a given time and space a unique unfolding of God's perfections as "othered"—outside of the infinite circle of the Trinity's self-giving that can never know any circumference.

It is in silence that the Christian learns as Moses to stand before the Burning Bush. We find our greatest struggle in becoming silent before God's silent love. It entails a letting go of the control we think we posses over our own life. It is a call to die to our false life in order to find our true life in the Other, dwelling intimately within us.

Nikos Kazantzakis describes how difficult it is for us to surrender to God:

> God is fire and you must walk on it . . . dance on it. At that moment the fire will become cool water. But until you reach that point, what a struggle, my Lord, what agony![4]

We need to turn into our "heart" and in silence we must enter deeply into ourselves and hear God Trinity, the Absolute Ground of all being, reveal to us through experiential knowledge, through enlightenment given by the Holy Spirit, that we are one with all being. Yet how reluctantly we are to return to that inner place of the heart to discover in the silencing of all our noises in our minds our true selves.

Dag Hammarskjold, the former Secretary-General of the United Nations, describes in his diary the difficulty of this journey inward:

> The longest journey
> is the journey inward
> Of him who has chosen his destiny
> Who has started his quest
> For the source of his being.[5]

SILENCING OUR HEART

If we are to meet God deeply at the core of our being, in our heart, as Scripture continually refers to that center within us, we must learn to silence our heart. What a lost art is this! We are drowning in a swirling ocean of noises all about us that tends to take us away from living at the center of our being. But how noisy are we within our minds and hearts! How agitated with thoughts, desires, fears, anxieties are we when we do come before the Lord in prayer!

The greater our distraction or diffusion, the less unifying is our union with God, "heart with heart." We of the Western culture are especially prone by our highly developed rational powers through science toward a chattering mind, like a cage of chattering monkeys. We find it very difficult to "let go" and surrender to a God that must be encountered through faith that presents him as dark, as in a mirror (1 Cor 13:12). We want to be the master, sure of ourselves. We are afraid to step out beyond the controls of our senses and our scientific method.

Yet God continually speaks to us from within our hearts: "Be still, and know that I am God" (Ps 46:10, KJV). God is always calling us into a silence of the heart where all artificiality crumbles, new psychic and spiritual powers burgeon forth and are released through the uncreated energies of God. Silence is the interior air that the spirit of our human nature needs in order to grow spiritually. Such silence leads us into the inner recess, and there our heavenly Father will recompense us.

When the disciples asked Jesus to teach them to pray, differently from reciting oral prayers of the Pharisees and Scribes on the street corners, he told them:

> But when you pray, go to your private room and, when you have shut your door, pray to your Father who is in that secret place, and your Father who sees all that is done in secret will reward you. (Mt 6:6)

THE RECOMPENSE OF THE FATHER

The Father recompenses anyone who seeks this inner, private room, the heart, and desires valiantly to stay there in the silence of surrendering love. This recompensing comes to us in the healing of psychic disturbances, the chaotic meaninglessness of so many past experiences that hang like dried skeletons within our memories, the anxieties that force us into an isolation of deadly loneliness. We become consoled and loved by God in an experience that is beyond any human concepts. We know that God loves us! This being-loved-by-God experience at the deepest level of our consciousness restores our inner strength and pushes us to new self-giving to God and neighbor in creative work.

PHYSICAL SILENCE

Silence takes place on several levels just as heart is a reality for us on various levels of meaning. Silence is the heart on these levels moving toward total integration of all our God-given powers. There is the silence on the physical, bodily level first. Here we need to learn how to bring an exterior silence into our bodies, our speech, the manner of our walking, our gestures, our general composure that radiates a deep interior centering. One cannot be centered deeply if one in continually babbling like a shallow mountain stream, not weighing our words and thoughts before the indwelling God.

St. Paul exhorts us to such inner physical and psychic silence that requires great vigilance and self-discipline through faith in the abiding presence of the risen Lord Jesus:

> Every thought is our prisoner, captured to be brought into obedience to Christ. Once you have given your complete obedience, we are prepared to punish any disobedience. (2 Cor 10:5)

Moving from noise to silence is always an uprooting, a leaving of something for something else. Yet there cannot be any movement into the inner silencing of the heart unless there be a movement away from physical noises that we allow our bodies to produce when we are not centered upon God as the Center of our being. "Your salvation lay in conversion and tranquillity, your strength in complete trust; and you would have none of it" (Is 30:15).

SILENCING THE MIND

This conversion consists in an inward turning, to attain an interior silence of the soul's faculties of memory, imagination, emotions, understanding, and will. Many persons seeking to become more prayerful have turned inwardly away from the noises of the physical world only to find deafening noises inside their minds. Great discipline of the mind is needed to uproot such noise and find an inner peace and tranquillity that can come only if our minds are focused more deeply upon God as the inner fortress of our strength. (In the next chapter we shall see how to silence the noises in our mind.)

St. Gregory of Nyssa of the fourth century captures well the value of centering all our soul-faculties upon God as the inner Center:

> So, too, I think, it is with the human mind. If it spreads itself out in all directions, constantly flowing our and dispersing to whatever pleases the senses, it will never have any notable force in its progress towards the true Good. But now recall the mind from all sides, and make it collect itself, so that itself, so that it may begin to operate in that function which is preferably connatural to it, without scattering and wasting itself: then the mind will find no obstacle in its rise to heaven and in its grasp of the true meaning of reality.[6]

NEED FOR DAILY SILENCE

Our silence and being alone with the Alone must become a living experience, some time during each day if we are to grow in deeper union with the indwelling Trinity. Such silence and solitude must be created in the heart in early morning before our day begins to unfold at its hectic pace and then again in the evening before retiring. Amidst our activities throughout the day we must learn to lift up our minds and hearts to God by re-touching that oneness with God as our Center living within us. It will be an interior desert that cries out for a new spring of lush fertility and new richness of life.

We will learn to stand before God in honesty, humility, silent to our own powers to tell God what we have been doing for him. It will be a period of stripping ourselves of all our artificial masks and rationalizations that we so easily hide behind during the day's activities. It will be a centering upon God as the Source of all our energies and desires. Soon we will look forward to such moments of silence and solitude.

The beginning of fears of being alone with God will soon yield to peace and even joy at "pulling" ourselves together before our Ultimate Concern. From focusing in utter silence upon God there will come over us an inner strength, equipping ourselves for the hectic activities of the day.

AVOIDING INNER SILENCE

We can easily see where the fault lies in our spiritual relationships with God and neighbor. It is because we do not think and act out of our true selves in God's living Word abiding within our hearts. We avoid turning deeply within ourselves and remaining in silence, because our illusory self seeks to hold on to the false securities that are truly insecurities, since they are the only world in which we have lived from early consciousness.

Our fragmented, sinful nature does not like to live in silence because silence has a way of revealing ourselves beyond all role playing and posturing before a God we believe, in our ignorance, we can manipulate to our ways of seeing reality. We pray with distractions and without force because we are afraid to our true selves in God's Word. We refuse to be ourselves by refusing to enter into silence in the depth of our hearts to experience an inner transformation by surrendering to the unseen God.

SPIRITUAL SILENCE

We have said that silence is more than mere physical silence, especially of speaking to God solely when we pray. True silence opens us up to an inner state of humility and poverty.

As the Spirit of God lets his light of truth shine upon our true selves, our unique person as enspirited and under the guidance of the Holy Spirit (Rm 8:15), we are filled with a spiritual sense of not only our nothingness and sinfulness before the beauty of the All-Holy. We die on the spirit-level to our false, worldly ego as we become broken in our spirit.

No longer is there the arrogant, self-assured human being who has been convinced that he or she has truly met the Lord in every rationalization and action done out of self-centeredness. We begin now to stand more habitually empty before the richness of God, a beggar with nothing to commend oneself. "My sacrifice is this broken spirit. You will not scorn this crushed and broken heart" (Ps 51:17).

We realize God cannot be manipulated any longer by ourselves. He must be approached with fear and trembling.

> God, examine me and know my heart,
> probe me and know my thoughts;
> make sure I do not follow pernicious ways,
> and guide me in the way that is everlasting. (Ps 139:23–24)

Poverty and silence coalesce before the awesome presence of the Lord that is revealed to the empty-handed. Silence teaches us that God must reveal himself to us and we must wait for him to speak. "Speak, Yahweh, your servant is listening" (1 Sm 3:9). "Behold the handmaid of the Lord; be it done unto me according to thy word" (Lk 1:38, KJV).

THE PARADOX OF SILENCE

What seems to be living in light when we live on the surface of our being is really to live in illusion and darkness. When we withdraw from noise and our own control over our lives and enter into a waiting, surrendering silence before God to speak his Word, we truly make a transition from darkness to light.

There comes to us a deeper awareness of hidden things. We
begin to move freely into the inner world of the invisible, but
yet most real. At first it seems to be our own weakness to
comprehend God and our true selves. But it becomes a keener
and keener realization as we persevere in inner silence. Bit is
because of God's great transcendence living within us that fills
us with an inner silence that becomes the most intense manner
of our communicating with God, not by doing anything, but
by becoming our true selves in his love by self-surrendering
love.

Merton captured the paradox of emptying silence in these
words:

> But true emptiness is that which transcends all things, and yet is
> immanent in all. For what seems to be emptiness in this case is
> pure being. It is not this, not that. Whatever you say of it, it is
> other than what you say. The character of emptiness, at least for
> a Christian contemplative, is pure love, true freedom. Love that
> is free of everything, not determined by any things or held down
> by any special relationship. It is a sharing, through the Holy
> Spirit, in the infinite charity of God. And so when Jesus told
> His disciples to love, He told them to love as universally as the
> Father who sends His rain alike on the just and the unjust. "Be
> ye perfect as Your heavenly Father." This purity, freedom and
> indeterminateness of love is the very essence of Christianity.[7]

TRANSITION FROM KNOWLEDGE ABOUT GOD TO LOVE

Darkness and silence are the realms of the indwelling
Trinity—Father, Son, and Spirit—living within and acting
lovingly through their uncreated energies of love. The Trinity,
God as a community of loving, self-sacrificing divine persons,
is the uncreated Ground of all being, the abyss of mystery that
exceeds all human knowledge. Yet the heavenly Father speaks
his Word, Jesus Christ, who is light, revelation, speech, and

meaning to us who wish to attune ourselves to his silent speaking of himself as Divine Word.

We must simply wait upon God's gratuitous gift of his Word, spoken when we surrender ourselves in the silencing of all our own powers to become through the working of the Holy Spirit receptivity before God's mysterious gift of love. To understand this basic paradox of hearing in silence the Word spoken by God, of seeing by not seeing, of darkness that is light, of "luminous darkness," and "sober inebriation" to quote St. Gregory of Nyssa, is to understand the movement of ourselves in our relations to God in a transition from knowledge to love. Knowledge that leads to love mingles God's transcendence and his immanence within our deepest cave: our heart.

For us to turn within and to accept the silence surrounding us as remote yet present, to accept our humility and poverty as part of our true existential being, but also to accept God's presence as loving and healing of our brokenness is to live in faith, graced by the ineffable presence of him who grounds all human reality. It is in the silenced heart that we learn to know that God is God, but also a community of an *I-Thou* in a *We* of persons, each giving himself in self-emptying love to us. As we discover through the illumination of the work of the Holy Spirit our heavenly Father in his imaged love through his only begotten Son, Jesus Christ, we are called to stretch upward to become always more our true selves as we paradoxically lose our false selves only to be birthed into greater oneness and yet greater uniqueness of a beautiful son or daughter of so loving a heavenly Father.

MEDITATION
BE STILL—I AM YOUR GOD

The aim of this meditation is to experience entering into inner silence on the body, soul, and spirit levels and experience your oneness in the indwelling Trinity.

1. *Silence On the Body Level.* Relax all parts of your body. Breathe deeply as we did in the meditation in Chapter 4. Breathe diaphragmatically. As you breathe in, feel the diaphragm muscle in the abdominal area extend itself outwardly. As you exhale slowly, feel the diaphragm seemingly move inward. Feel that basic rhythm, so much like the ebb and flow of the ocean tide. Close your eyes and concentrate on all the individual parts of your body. Start with the top of your head, the forehead, the eyelids. Relax the tension in the nerves of your eyes, your cheeks, your chin. Let your shoulders relax without sagging. Concentrate on your chest, heart area, abdomen, the genital area. Relax your arms, elbows, wrists, hands, fingers. Let go of the tenseness in your hips, thighs, knees, calves, ankles, and toes. Believe by faith as you let go of any tension that God is present in all parts of your body, that your body is a temple of God. Breathe deeply and enjoy that loving presence of the triune God within you. Let go of the control of your life and experience the pulsating energies of the love of God within you. Desire to surrender your entire being in return to God in childlike, trusting love.

2. *Silence On the Mind Level.* Still your mind of the many images, phantasms, thoughts, worries, and fears by a descending movement into your *heart,* that core or center of your being that is the center of your gravity deep down around your pelvic area.

Picture in your mind that you are on the twentieth floor of a large building. You enter an elevator that takes you slowly down into the basement. As you see yourself passing the various floors from the twentieth to the basement floor, feel yourself sinking down below your rational control in your mental activities that brings you into a oneness with the Trinity dwelling in the darkness of your heart, that surrenders the seeming light of your controlling reason.

Stop at each floor, each level of your consciousness, and tell yourself that you are becoming more relaxed, more centered upon the indwelling Father, Son, and Spirit: 20–19–18–

17–1–0. God is your strength, and you are touching the Trinity. You are totally relaxed and at peace.

3. *Silence On the Spirit Level.* Breathe in and out rhythmically and begin to think your Christian mantra: "Be still!" as you breathe in; "I am your God" as you breathe out. Repeat, lengthening your breathing, as you maintain your relaxation.

Feel yourself becoming integrated as a whole person, a child of God, as you surrender yourself totally into the loving hands of the Father, through his Son, Jesus, in the Spirit of Love.

6

A Broken Heart

In that delightful modern odyssey into the inner world of expanded consciousness of Carlos Castaneda in his book *Journey to Ixtlan,* Don Juan, the Indian shaman or spiritual guide, teaches his disciple the necessity of becoming a warrior. Such a warrior does not fear the enemies of the desert that might destroy him. Rather he has so much *élan vital,* such a verve to live fully, that he bravely attacks the enemies that might threaten his promise of greater life.

The master teaches the disciple how to enter into the desert and how to listen in silence to the real world for the first time. Therein doing the battle of forces around him, he would begin to see what was always there, but which most people fail to see. Don Juan explains:

> What stopped inside you yesterday was what people have been telling you the world is like. You see, people tell us from the time that we are born that the world is such and such and so and so, and naturally we have no choice but to see the world the way people have been telling us it is.[1]

One must be alert, courageous, and trained to deal with the full existential realm of the interior life. If the individual is ill-prepared for the plunge into this deeper level of expanded consciousness, it will be totally self-destructive. One needs a spiritual director, guru, shaman, or roshi. The names differ, but their roles are always the same. It is for this reason that every form of mysticism within a fixed religion has insisted strongly on a "spirit-filled" person, capable from his or her own experiences to traverse the circuitous ways of the interior life and from experiential knowledge of human nature and the study of Holy Scripture and theology to beget the disciple into the life of the Spirit.

For the Christian mystic, the one who wishes to live at the center of his/her true being in transcendent union with the Source of all Being, there is a need to be able to discern the authentic workings of the Holy Spirit from the evil spirits that so easily introduce "tares" where the Divine Sower sowed only good seeds. The greatest function of a spiritual guide is to warn the neophyte against the pitfalls of the inner world and to encourage the disciple against the threat of what Paul Tillich calls "non-being."

NON-BEING

Any of the states of expanded consciousness bring the anxiety of non-being. Tillich writes in his book *The Courage to Be*:

> Basic anxiety is the anxiety of a finite being about the threat of non-being. . . . Actualization of being implies the ability to take courageously upon oneself the anxiety of non-being.[2]

For this reason Don Juan instructs his disciple, Carlos Castaneda: "The apprenticeship is long and arduous . . . in order to withstand the impact of such an encounter."[3]

The Christian life has been described by Jesus Christ and his disciples as a death-unto-life experience. He described this life as a denial of one's self, as a shouldering of one's cross and following him (Mt 10:38; 16:24; Mk 8:34; Lk 9:23;

14:27). Jesus insisted that the seed had to fall into the earth and die before it could bring forth greater fruit (Jn 12:24). Nicodemus was told by Jesus that he had to be reborn from above in order to enter into the Kingdom of Heaven (Jn 3:3–5).

LAW OF INNER GROWTH

But this is to describe the law of inner growth in all human lives. Made according to God's own image and likeness (Gn 1:26–27), we possess the ability to stretch ourselves upward to attain new levels of transcendent meaningfulness by letting go of lower levels of being. Holy Scripture presents this conversion process in terms of an *exodus,* a passing-over to a state of becoming progressively free in the darkness and sterility of the desert that leads to the promised land.

Psychologists speak of it as a twofold movement. The first stage consists of accepting ourselves with honesty and without excuse. This is an awakening moment, revealing the truth that what we thought was our true personhood was in reality a false self. Many of us seek various ways of escaping this self-knowledge, such as great business with work or travel, or becoming couch potatoes.

Only if we learn to accept sincerely our existential self can we ever hope to open up to the second movement: namely, to hunger and thirst in the totality of our being; to be someone more noble, more loving, more in our oneness with God and neighbor and the entire universe. This is the élan toward new life. This is True Being calling us to experience our true selves in the Source as a unique manifestation of God's presence in human form on this earth.

But this can only follow the letting go of the false self and all the protective devices and techniques we have been using to secure the lie that that illusory person is the true self. And how most of us human beings detest the thought of the dying process that will yield to new life! How we are afraid to enter into the depths of our unconscious in order that we might become more conscious of our beautiful, unique self as we bring the brokenness in our heart to the healing power of Love itself.

BREAKING THE FALSE IDOLS

This conversion experience can also be described in terms of prayer, for every true conversion to living according to more transcendent values can come about only through the ultimate loving power that allows us to let go and surrender ourselves into his caring hands. In the initial stages of prayer we needed God, but we created him according to our own images and needs. He was to satisfy all of our creaturely needs, and, in fact, to help us retain that false self we lived for so many years.

The transitional point comes when we can look earnestly at our selves and begin to accept the fact that there is something false, unreal, inauthentic in the way we approach God. When we silence our hearts we not only have a burning desire to leave the husks of swine and claim our divine inheritance help out to us by our heavenly Father through his Son and Holy Spirit, but we are also forced to confront a heart-consciousness of our brokenness. This brokenness deep within us seemingly rises up as darkness to eclipse the delicate light that would lead us to true freedom, transfiguration, and divinization into our unique, true self, our essential self, that self that manifests God's beauty in earthly form.

In the words of Gabriel Marcel, such a person "has become once and for all a question for himself."[4] The most important question we must ask ourselves daily is: Will we stay inside ourselves, groping for ways in which we can let God be truly God instead of running "outside" to be diverted from the call to new life? Marcel describes the feeling of inner emptiness that comes to the person who courageously looks inside:

> When we are at rest, we find ourselves almost inevitably put in the presence of our own inner emptiness, and this very emptiness is in reality intolerable to us. But there is more, there is the fact that through this emptiness we inevitably become aware of the misery of our condition, a "condition so miserable," says Pascal, "that nothing can console us when we think about it carefully." Hence the necessity of diversion.[5]

Such an emptiness within reveals in an amazing burst of light inside of darkness how dishonest we have been toward God in our prayer. We see how we have hidden behind doctrines and liturgical rituals—structures of our religious or spiritual life that served to guarantee both a false security and a closing off to God's continued call to deeper conversion.

Now through a deepening faith we have the courage to look at our habitual attitude toward God. Shame fills our hearts at the brazenness of how we have used God for our own selfish purposes. Need, not true love, was behind most of our prayer life. Now prayer becomes a desire to crash down the false idols, the images and words used to present ourselves to God as though we were his equals, or worse, that he is an object, at our beck and call.

The working of God's Spirit of grace to instill into us anxiety, fear, and disgust as we confront our existence in the light of our "non-being" is not merely a self-centered reflection on death. It is an ontological "nostalgia" to rise from such a deathly condition and return home to discover our true selves in the passionate love of our heavenly Father. It is to be in love with our Father in total self-surrendering trust.

THE DAIMONIC

We cannot understand the religious meaning of the term "heart" unless we also see that out of the "heart" also "come evil intentions: murder, adultery, fornication, theft, perjury, slander. These are the things that make a man unclean" (Mt 13:19–20), as Jesus preached. The ancient Greeks referred to the *daemon* or *daimoni* within all of us. There are light and darkness coexisting in our hearts, the already beautiful, unique, loving, true person with our "essential" *I*, always being drawn by the Holy Spirit into greater conscious awareness of oneness with the Absolute Being, and also simultaneously the false or worldly ego.

The great German poet Rainer Maria Rilke (†1926) expressed the two faces of the same coin when he wrote: "If my devils are to leave me, I am afraid my angels will take flight as well."[6]

DEVIL AND SYMBOL

We can perhaps understand this relationship by going to the root meaning of "devil" (*diabolos* in Greek) and "symbol." *Diabolos* literally means to tear apart (*dia-bollein*). The opposite of diabolic is "symbolic," which is derived from the Greek verb *sym-bollein,* to throw together or unite. Dr. Rollo May, the popular American author and psychoanalyst, gives us a keen insight in his explanation of the *daimonic:*

> There lie in these words tremendous implications with respect to an ontology of good and evil. The symbolic is that which draws together, ties, integrates the individual in himself and with his group; the diabolic, in contrast, is that which disintegrates and tears apart. Both of these are present in the daimonic.[7]

A PART OF A BROKEN WORLD

From Scripture and human history we learn that we form a solidarity with the whole world in our brokenness, in "the sin of the world." We find our darkness to be a part of the world's darkness. We have inherited it simply by being a part of the human race. With King David, we can all confess before God and other human beings: "You know I was born guilty, a sinner from the moment of conception" (Ps 51:5).

But you and I are individual persons who have become what we are and what we will be through our actions upon and reactions to other individual persons. Our parents, friends, teachers, wife, husband, children, enemies, and even "indifferent" acquaintances have helped to make us what we are by their attitudes, acts, and even omissions. It is here in our "heart," both in the conscious and unconscious layers of our body, soul, and spirit levels, that we come face to face with the *daimonic* in all of us, that which is part of our broken state of inauthenticity and also that which explains the good and the creative in our lives with its great potential for even such greater beauty in the future, depending on our free cooperation with God's grace.

INTERRELATIONSHIPS

We can only grow in greater self-consciousness and hence in an awareness of ourselves as an individual *I,* capable of self-giving in true love, by relationships with other centers of consciousness, able to call us into being by their love given freely to us. We grow in a society, a stable group of human beings in communication with each other. St. Paul could write: "The life and death of each of us has its influence on others" (Rm 14:7). Like Tennyson's *Ulysses,* in all of our travels from the first moment of waking consciousness until this present moment and even to the end of our earthly existence, we can say: "I am a part of all that I have met."

The interdependence on others, not only for our being, but for our being such and such a person, is testified to today by microbiology. We inherit in birth not only the values of our parents, but through them the values of generations and generations that preceded them. What an amazing world of interrelationships science opens up to us! Each of the 100 trillion cells in our body contains about 100,000 different genes, composed of DNA (deoxyribonucleic acid). Each DNA molecule stores coded information to be used to sustain and duplicate itself. Through such dependency upon our parents, we receive more than similar physical traits; we are also the recipients of much of their positive and negative qualities. We share in the brokenness even before we see the light of day.

NOT FREE TO LOVE

We crave above all else in life to love and to be loved. But pitifully the mounting rate of lonely persons committing physical or psychological suicides, the increase of broken marriages that end in divorce after divorce, the inability of so many parents to relate lovingly to their children and children to their parents, all point out how unfree we human beings are to love and receive love.

What inner brokenness we experience in what God meant to be both the most human and divine experience for us—namely, human love! We sincerely tell our loved ones that we really want to love them. But as we learn to enter into the depths of ourselves and others, opening ourselves in all of our "unmasked" self, we experience fears and doubts. We find a true confrontation with our unredeemed, hidden areas that come out as we see ourselves being mirrored in the openness of the other.

Demands of sensitivity and fidelity not known before are made as we receive the gift of the other. Self can no longer be the center, but we must seek humbly to serve only the unique godliness in the other. True love makes the terrifying demand on us to let the other be completely him/herself. My selfish needs must yield to the godly desire to seek only to serve the uniqueness in the other, that which will fulfill the other's true self.

But what agony to let go and not hold on to the other! What a fear as my unreal self battles the hidden real self, as I struggle to "use" the other or die to the false in me to "serve" the other! I can so easily insist that the other person measure up to my expectations that means all too often to satisfy my selfish needs. In my selfishness I can lose the "symbolic," that which integrates and binds into a oneness, and I yield to the "diabolic," that which dis-integrates and scatters.

I can lose the sense of wonder mystery, poetry and its going beyond my falsely constructed demands and insist that the other person be more the father or mother that I once needed to touch me and cuddle me.

THE PAIN OF PRAYER

Human love is true prayer when we learn to die to our self-centeredness in order to open up to the creative presence of God in another. But in both true human love and prayer (can we truly separate the two: love of God and neighbor?), there is so much necessary pain. In both, if there is to be any progress, there must be a touching of two centers of consciousness and this always means pain.

In prayer, especially, we are driven by God's Spirit into the barren desert of our inner self, in e depths of our heart. Like Jesus, we are to encounter the *daimonic* in us, both the horrible areas of darkness, fear, brokenness, and the possibility of new, resurrectional light, new life to come forth as creative energy released when the darkness is confronted and transformed into light.

It takes courage to go deeper into ourselves to confront the dark side in our heart. And for this reason, the majority of us in prayer stay up "on top" in a very controlled relationship with God and the person that we think we are, but that is not the real person that God wishes to love. We fear encountering so much ugliness in forms of darkness, painful memories, and distortions.

We fear the great temptation to push deeper into the unknown. Perhaps our small skiff on such troubled waters of the unconscious will easily capsize. Can we be sure that, going so deeply within ourselves, we will be able to return? The line is very thin between madness and ecstatic union with God.

But farther into our brokenness we must go. The figures within us taunt us and attack us with a fierceness that breaks all of our ego-power. We feel helpless, trapped, surrounded by the most hideous enemies the human mind could every imagine. Are they real or are they illusion? What is real and what is unreal? Jesus Christ, come to my rescue! Have mercy on me, the greatest of all sinners!

The false posturing before God, the grand soliloquies that I have been directing to the ear of God all fall from my heart as so many dry leaves falling from trees that in autumn no longer have need of them. What I thought was important and significant in my life—fame, honor, pleasure, the joys shared with friends—all seem truly like straw. How unimportant they all seem! How unimportant I seem in my self-controlled worldly ego!

THE INNERMOST SELF

Whatever be the skein of knotted, twisted threads that have fashioned the tapestry of our lives (and so many of such influences were beyond our personal control), there lies deep within us another self, that true self of unrealized potentiality. In our brokenness we are driven into our creaturely nothingness. What can we do to extricate ourselves from the overpowering forces that have mostly come originally from without, but now lie like unchained, wild dogs within us?

Such a confrontation with our inner brokenness and nothingness before such overwhelming forces of negativity and destructive force can be the turning point to a new life, a life of crying out for God's mercy and healing. Psychologist Dr. William Kraft speaks of our existential grasping of our nothingness in forms of loneliness, aloneness, depression, anxiety, guilt, frustration, anger, boredom, apathy, and anguish.[8]

Deep within us lies our real self, the person unrealized as yet, but loved infinitely by the triune God. God's Spirit hovers over this chaos, the darkness that could blaze forth into creative light, peace, and joy. If we could only stretch out and follow that thin, silvery streak of godly light out of the binding slavery into true freedom. It is here in our true self that God dwells, making his mansion (Jn 14:23), as we become more and more spirit, communicating freely unto intimate loving communion with God's Spirit.

GOD'S HEALING LOVE

To live on this level of loving union with the indwelling Trinity is to burst the bonds of predeterministic forces from within us and to step out of the cave of crippling, stifling darkness into the bright day of spring. Only God is powerful enough to aid us in becoming "reborn" again in his Holy Spirit of love (Jn 3:3–5). Only in experiencing the healing love from a tender, loving Mother-Father God, made manifest through the Spirit of the risen Jesus, can we rise from e brokenness of our past experiences to embrace new levels of a life in Christ, which is, as God always intended, to become our real self in the Word made flesh.

No longer do we have to be locked in the prison of our narcissism, to obey the dictates of others as the sole criterion of truth. Our habitual, low profile, with all of our defenses to cover up our hurting inadequacies is replaced by an authentic humility that shows us our true selves from God's view in the light of God's special gifts and endowments. Honesty and sincerity become like two bright shining beacons that dissipate any self-deceit from whatever cause.

This is a call to live in the freedom of the children of God. But it is a frightening call that demands daily courage to encounter the *daimonic* forces of darkness and to develop a new potential for greater aliveness to God's loving presence everywhere. Dr. Carl Rogers described this freedom:

> Freedom to be oneself is a frighteningly responsible freedom, and an individual moves toward it cautiously, fearfully, and with almost no confidence at first.[9]

It is within ourselves, into our heart that we must enter in honesty and poverty of spirit—that is, the silence needed to hear God speak his still-pointed Word. Into the tomb of our inner darkness, the light of God's tender love bursts upon us. Tears of sorrow and repentance, tears of fright at our own *nonbeing* pour forth gently as God's soft, healing dew falls upon the cracked, parched earth of our heart to stir those seeds of new life into reality.

As we utter the words, "Have mercy on me, O God, in your goodness" (Ps 51:1), we continually hear his healing response that thrills us into new life: "This child of mine was dead and has come back to life; he was lost and is found" (Lk 15:24).

PRAYER-EXERCISE

As you enter into the cave of your heart, allow the images of this poetic meditation to flow gently like soothing, clean spring water over the brokenness that you discover lying within your heart as skeletons of the past. Surrender your inner darkness and the forces inside your heart that rise up and hold you mercilessly in bondage, preventing you from becoming free to walk in the newness of God's healing love in Christ Jesus.

THE CAVE OF MY HEART

I walked along the quiet mountain road.
The full moon laughed with joy
while the rest of nature slept.
I entered into a crevice
of a rock near the stream.

There was peace.
But then I felt God's presence
slowly come upon me.
Faster and faster He pursued me.
I wasn't running from Him.
I was entering into Him!

Deeper and deeper
I plunged!
I knew that somehow
when I left this place
I would always remain
in that crevice,
so full of God's peace and joy.

I had touched God.
I had found Heaven on earth!
God's Spirit had come upon me
in that moonlit evening
as I hid in the arms
of God, my Beloved!

Oh, what healing Love
comes over my brokenness!
All healing comes from God
in the desert cave
when I, in brokenness,
call out to You, Divine Physician.

I will never be the same
since You touched me
and I hid in Your healing arms.
New powers awake
as spring-clarion sounds
within the depths of that crevice,
the rock of my heart.

Locked-in petals
of a bedewed rose
gently let go
to unveil a new harmony
of many things captured,
in the union of one flower
of exquisite beauty.

The chaotic past, dried bones
of long yester-years,
receive the soft breath
of God's Spirit of Love,
and they become enfleshed
into a living being.

I come out of the past
as I cry to my Lord:
"Lord, Jesus Christ, Son of God,
have mercy on me,
a sinner."

Like butterfly bursting
forth in melted gold
with wet, tightly packed wings,
I stretch upward.

Dry wings strengthen
and lift me aloft
to new, dizzying heights
of union with God.

But then I hear
that healing voice
say to me,
"Go to your broken
brothers and sisters.
Stretch out your hands
on their pain-ridden bodies.

Give My healing Love
to all that you meet.
Be My hands and feet,
that can, like the Shepherd,
gather again the scattered sheep
and bring them to My Father."

Broken by healed,
I step out in faith
to be a broken healer
to a broken world.[10]

G.A.M.

7

A Heart Healed by Divine Love

In a scene from the popular musical *Jesus Christ Superstar,* Jesus finds himself in a deserted, rocky place. Out of the caves and holes in the rocks crawl the lepers, the blind, and crippled, seeking to touch him and be healed. Jesus is deluged, sucked down into the mass of broken humanity. As the sick claw at him, Jesus screams: "It's too much! There are too many of you!"

Jesus the Light came into our darkness. He carried within himself the fullness of God's life and wholeness. He came among us to share in his abundant life. "I have come so that they may have life and have it to the full" (Jn 10:10).

The one great sin for us human beings is to live in the darkness of our own isolated loneliness. We were made for loving union with God and all human beings. But sin forces us to resort to power as the means to move out of our self-absorption and loneliness. We seek by many so-called "sinful" actions to empower ourselves into a proper acceptance by others. Yet pitifully such approaches lead us farther and farther from true love and our true selves as God's manifestation of beauty in this world.

Jesus' redemptive power is one of removing our ignorance by giving us through his Holy Spirit an abiding experience of the heavenly Father's great love as indwelling us as in a mansion, a temple (Jn 14:23). Jesus spoke to those who heard him during his lifetime on earth and he still speaks to us through the Gospel stories.

But it was not what he said that touched hearts and healed them. It was his loving presence that could touch the sick and the sinful, that could gaze upon them and mirror for them the infinite love of the Father. He stirred up the image of himself locked in each person he met and called it into its true being. He was the Son of God, and he loved the son and daughter of God in each person he met.

> Yes, God loved the world so much that he gave his only Son, so that everyone who believes in him may not be lost but may have eternal life. (Jn 3:16)

JESUS: GOD'S HEALING MERCY AND LOVE

The Good News that God was preparing his people for was the final revelation of his burning love for them. Isaiah and Jeremiah had foretold the new times when tears would be wiped away and sorrow would be no more. God's revealing Love stood before those suffering and was filled with compassion, seeing how they were held in bondage and sickness: "And when he saw the crowds, he felt sorry for them because they were harassed and dejected, like sheep without a shepherd" (Mt 9:36).

In Jesus, God forgives all our offenses and cures all our diseases (Ps 103:3). God's mercy that is above all his works (Ps 145:9) becomes incarnated in Jesus of Nazareth. It would be only when he suffers and dies, ignominiously emptied out on the cross, that Jesus would become the living Word of God's healing presence among us.

The whole of Jesus' public life was to manifest the tender, merciful love of God for his suffering children. At times Jesus manifests a reticence to demonstrate his power to heal. At other times he appeals to his miracles and healings as signs of his oneness with the Father. These are not weak vacillations in Jesus' character. His primary work, his hour, was to become the fullness of God's communicating, loving presence to mankind. He would not be sidetracked by any vain glory as a miracle worker or healer. He was merely the Word spoken by God.

Yet because he was so much one with the Father, seeing the maimed, the blind, the lepers and the paralytics, the epileptics and the possessed, the sinners bound by hatred for others, by lust and pride, he, as it were, could not but be compassionate, full of mercy and loving as his Father is. Throughout his whole public ministry, Jesus' loving concern for his children was in the image of his Father. He knew what forces of evil were seeking to destroy God's people. And wherever he saw the power of darkness covering mankind, he burned with zeal to bring the light of God's love to destroy the effects of sin.

JESUS THE LIBERATOR

We believe in the power of the Word of God. What Jesus did, as recorded in the Gospel, he continues to do for all who wish to accept him as the God-Man, the Redeemer and Savior, the healing Lord. Like Lazarus, all of us are bound. And Jesus wishes to unbind us and set us free. He still performs his saving role of freeing us. "You will learn the truth and the truth will make you free. . . . So if the Son makes you free, you will be free indeed" (Jn 8:32).

Jesus literally set the captives free, in fulfillment of Isaiah's prophecy (Is 61:1), when he healed the sick and the broken, the diseased or mentally unbalanced, those caught up in self-ishness and unlove. Nor does he consider those he healed as healthy only when their sins were forgiven or when their bodies were restored to physical health. Jesus came to give them health holistically on all levels of their being—body, soul, and spirit. It was the whole person that Jesus loves and to whom he ministers his life.

FULL HEALING

The full healing for all of us comes only through the illumination of our minds and hearts by the Spirit of Jesus who dies for love of us. When the Son of Man was lifted up, he became a freeing power for all of us from every kind of demonic possession or sickness. Jesus refers to himself on the cross as the serpent that Moses fashioned of bronze and raised on high. Everyone who was bitten by crawling serpents, looking upon the raised serpent of bronze, would be healed and would live (Nm 11:4–9).

> And the Son of Man must be lifted up as Moses lifted up the serpent in the desert, so that everyone who believes may have eternal life in him. (Jn 3:13–14)

In our brokenness, when we are not in God's life, living fully in the likeness of his Son, we are outside God's Kingdom. Just as Jesus preached the Good News that the Kingdom was breaking in upon each person who would receive him as Savior and Healer, so he touches us in prayer and leads us into the Kingdom relationships with his Father through the Holy Spirit of Love. Jesus still heals all who open themselves to his love, which is the "imaged" love of our very heavenly Father as Jesus teaches: "As the Father has loved me, so I have loved you" (Jn 15:9).

LOVE HEALS

What wonderful consolation to know by his Spirit that both he and the Father have come and made their home within us

(Jn 14:23). This is what the Kingdom of God is all about. God's eternal love, personalized in the intimate relations of Father, Son, and Holy Spirit, touching us in that intercommunication that we call prayer, draws us out of our isolation and impersonal loneliness to enter into the very family of God.

In such moments of prayerful communion with God within us, the power of sin and death is broken. Jesus truly lives and walks into our lives, the same, but now gloriously risen Lord, and performs the same signs announcing the Kingdom of God.

> I am the resurrection.
> If anyone believes in me, even though he dies he will live,
> and whoever lives and believes in me
> will never die.
> Do you believe this? (Jn 11:25–26)

Jesus still asks us: "Do you really believe that I am the imaged love of the Father? Do you believe I can heal you and bring you into full health as I did all those whom I encountered during my earthly life, provided only that they believed in me?" Or perhaps that more fundamental and urgent question is: Are we aware that we are sick and desperately in need of healing? Do we realize we are not living according to our full potential, the full life that God created us to enjoy and with which to praise and glorify him?

William of St. Thierry in the twelfth century wrote in his treatise *On the Solitary Life*:

> Although in sinning, [human] nature rejected order, and departed from the integrity of its original state; if it turns back towards God, it will recover immediately, according to the measure of fear and love it shows him, all it had lost in turning away from him. How agreeable it would be, and in principle how easy, to live according to *nature*, if only our foolishness would allow us to do so. Cure man of his folly, and immediately his nature would be able to look on the things of Nature without fear.[1]

Bernard Lonergan expresses what it means to love God who dwells within us and allows us to transcend our "unnatural" self by discovering our true, transcendent self in God's love:

> To be in love is to be in love with someone. To be in love without qualifications or conditions or reservations or limits is to be in love with someone transcendent. When someone transcendent is my beloved, he is in my *heart*, real to me from within me. When that love is the fulfillment of my unrestricted thrust to self-transcendence through intelligence and truth and responsibility, the one that fulfills that thrust must be supreme in intelligence, truth, goodness, Since he chooses to come to me by a gift of love for him, he himself must be love. Since loving him is my transcending myself, it also is a denial of the self to be transcended.
>
> Since loving him means loving attention to him, it is prayer, mediation, contemplation. Since love of him is fruitful, it overflows into love of all those that he loves or might love. Finally, from an experience of love focused on mystery there wells forth a longing for knowledge, while love itself is a longing for union; so for the lover of the unknown beloved that concept of bliss is knowledge of him and union with him, however they may be achieved.[2]

We were created by God to be whole persons, totally integrated in all body, soul, and spirit levels of relationships. We were to find our relationship to the godly within us insofar as we had a mind, an intellect, and a will, to know and receive God's great love for ourselves. If we , as planned by God in the first Adam and actualized in Jesus, the New Adam, were to live according to our "essential self," according to our true nature, freely consenting to love God in loving service, we would be in harmony within ourselves. We would be in good health also with God and with the whole world around us.

But sin brought death to the God-life in us. We were plunged into a disorientation from God and the world around us. Evil is not an objective entity existing by itself. It is an illusion of what we in sin were never meant to be. It is an unreal condition that we, also, so often assume to be our "natural" self.

St. Gregory of Nyssa described the condition of a human person living in sin:

> The lofty has been brought low: what was made in the image of heaven as been reduced to earth; he who was ordained to rule has been enslaved; what was created for immortality has been destroyed by death. . . . he who was familiar with impassability has been transformed into a life of passion and death.[3]

BODILY HEALING

All of us can usually detect when we are in need of physical healing. The body is an organic mechanism. Parts deteriorate. Viruses attack and bring infection into the bloodstream. Vitality slows down as we grow older. Our senses diminish in strength. Our vision and hearing usually grow weaker as we advance beyond middle age. And so our aches and pains cry out for freeing for healing, for restoration to former strength.

We must believe that God is interested in our bodily health. Jesus came as God's image in human form. He never turned away the blind, the lame, the crippled, the lepers, and the paralytics, but he healed all who believed in his power to set them free from their physical slavery to bodily sickness and disease.

> He went round the whole of Galilee teaching in their synagogues, proclaiming the Good News of the kingdom and curing all kinds of diseases and sickness among the people. His fame spread throughout Syria, and those who were suffering from

diseases and painful complaints of one kind or another, the possessed, epileptics, the paralyzed, were all brought to him,. and he cured them (Mt 4:23–24; 9:35).

This same Jesus, risen in glory, still brings his healing love to mend our broken bodies. It is not that he sees the body as something distinct from one's soul or spirit. So now, as in his lifetime, Jesus, the image of the loving Father, is filled with love and compassion for all of us not free from sickness and disease of any kind. He sees us as whole persons with very particular bodies.

PHYSICAL HEALING

Yet Jesus, the Divine Physician, knows better than our modern doctors how the body, soul and spirit interact in us. These are not tightly concealed compartments of self-contained entities. About seventy to seventy-five percent of our physical diseases are rooted in psychic suggestions received into the unconscious until the consciousness uses our autonomic system to create the sickness that "acts " out the inner psychic suggestion.

We all have daily experience of the increasing stresses and anxieties that we must live under, and we know how such psychic factors powerfully affect our bodies. High blood pressure, heart condition, ulcers, allergies, arthritis, even stages of cancer development[4] show a direct relationship between a disturbed psyche and certain somatic diseases and illnesses.

Scientists have shown that our minds are capable of producing great electromagnetic energy fields that influence the human, bodily organism as well as other living organisms such as plants and animals. Experiments have been conducted in Yoga, Zen Buddhism, Transcendental Meditation, Silva Mind-Control, hypnosis, and biofeedback that have shown conclusively how mental activities can produce great changes in the physiological state.

God has revealed much about the workings of the human psyche through the discoveries made in depth-psychology and psychotherapy. One of Carl Jung's commentators, Dr. Ira Progoff, compares the psyche to a cross-sectional drawing of geologic rock formation. At the top is a thin layer of surface rock that we call *consciousness*. Below this is a thicker layer of rock that we call *personal unconscious*. Underlying both of these layers there is a dark, volcanic base extending back to the very core of the earth itself, bringing the individual into primordial contact with all of creation as a part to the whole. This Jung calls the *collective unconscious* or conscience of the Universal Man. Occasionally out of this volcano there erupt materials that rise to the surface, passing through the other layers.[5]

PSYCHIC BROKENNESS

If we are to attain an integrated personality, to harmonize all the various levels of psychic life within our mind (Jung calls this process "individuation") the upper layers of the psyche must be harmonized with the lower layers. This means that the lower layers must be opened up to the scrutiny of the consciousness. We will remain crippled psychically and will always be the victim of primordial factors in our life unless we open up these lower layers to inner healing.

But when we allow ourselves in moments of deep relaxation, inner silence, and transcendent prayer to go within and see what lies beyond the superficial level of our controlled consciousness, which in fact Carl Jung calls the area of the unconscious, we find an inner psychic world crying out for healing and harmony. Society with its "proper" way that we should act in certain circumstances, not doing some things just because it is not the agreed custom, does help us in this external control. But beneath this "properness," all too often we

find a seething volcano of self-love, hatred toward certain individuals, readiness to use violence to get our own way.

The jungle is very much within us underneath the external
polish of an educated person. The *Lord of the Flies* is experienced by all of us if we have any reflective self-knowledge at
all.

FEAR OF FEAR

One of the greatest psychic enslavements is fear. It is the
opposite of faith that pours into our spirit as a gift of God's
Spirit of love. When we lack such a healing experience of
God's personal, indwelling love for us, we lack a sense of true
identity. Fear is primarily centered in the apprehension of a
future danger, unhappiness, doubt, anxiety, worry, dread,
hatred, anger, horror, fright, or terror. The thought of an
impending evil weighs heavily upon our psyche and our body,
crippling our growth, and breaking down our health.

Fear can be about innumerable objects. It is the state of
fear from which we must be delivered, for often the objects that
we fear are only in our minds. The nation's number one health
problem lies in the area of emotional and mental illnesses. And
most of these psychic disturbances are due to needless fear.
Most doctors are concerned with bringing a healing to the
effects of fear. But we must discover the root of fear that is so
often centered in a lack of faith and trust in God's loving care
for us.

FEAR NOT

Jesus came to reveal to us that we have a loving Father who
numbers every hair on our heads. We are not to worry in the
light of this great revelation, for if God takes care of the birds
of the air and clothes the lilies of the fields, now much more,
Jesus insists, will our Father in Heaven take care of all future
needs? The conclusion is, therefore, "There is no need to be

afraid, little flock, for it has pleased your Father to give you the kingdom" (Lk 12:32).[6]

We say, "Yes, Lord, I believe," yet we then begin to fear new areas of the unknown. This cripples us, preventing us from living dynamic, decisive lives because we are stalemated in a no-decision attitude. We wait for others to move us into positions where all freedom to make determined decisions out of our true selves is taken away. Or at least we find the field of choices narrowed down by our fearful inactivity. Such slavery removes us from the full life Jesus came to bring us.

We must seek the causes of fear and then bravely eliminate them by firm, rational action. We become liberated from the bondage of fear when we can look at fear itself in terms, not only of our own strength but, above all, the strength of God. If fear has come from our own consciousness or unconscious, it will be dissolved by pouring into those psychic areas the healing power of God's personalized, uncreated energies of love dwelling actively within our heart at the core of our being. By God's Spirit we will see God's vision of reality that will dispel the projections of the insecure false ego.

But the central question is: "Are we ready and willing to let go of these fears that allow us an enslaving 'comfort' and security instead of pushing into the dark world of deeper faith?" To let go of such fears is a true dying process that many of us are not quite ready to make. That is to say, many of us prefer living in the cave of fearful shadows brought about by self-centered projections instead of surrendering affectionately in childlike faith to the indwelling Trinity.

HEALING OF THE SPIRIT

In 1930 Carl Jung wrote a statement that loses nothing of its force and truth for the many years that have passed since then:

> During the past 30 years, people from all the civilized countries of the earth have consulted me. . . . Among my patients in the second half of life—that is to say, over thirty-five, there has not been one whose problem in the last resort was not that of finding a religious outlook on life. It is safe to say that every one of them fell ill because he had lost that which the living religions of every age have given to their followers, and none of them has been really healed who has not regained this religious outlook.[7]

How can we become liberated from our own projections and the world we have been so busy creating in order to live in what we consider the "really real world," that God has never had a part in creating? How can we enter into the radical healing of our intimate relationships with God, neighbor, and the entire, material cosmos around us? We have already pointed out the need for inner silence, for constant vigilance over every thought and over our imagination to bring such under "captivity and in obedience to Jesus Christ" as St. Paul writes (2 Cor 10:5). We need to look at ourselves through the illumination of the Holy Spirit on all levels of our brokenness and disunity away from living at the center of the core of our being in Christ.

We need, again through the power of the Holy Spirit, to have a healthy disgust for ourselves, a nostalgia such as the prodigal son experienced as he fed the swine and pondered his separation from his loving father (Lk 15:11ff). Then we will experience tears of true repentance pouring out, like soft rain falling on the hard earth to soften it. The shell around our false world splits, and God's penetrating love filters into our hearts to stir into new life the great potential lying there.

Dr. Karlfried Graf Dürckheim describes this new consciousness:

> Freed from his small ego—releases from pride, from the desire to dominate, the fear of pain, the longing for security—he becomes firmly anchored in his true centre. Thus centred, he is

able to be receptive to the forces of Being which, with or without his awareness, transform, support, shape and protect him while at the same time enabling him to reveal these forces to the world by the quality of his work, his ability to create and his capacity for love.[8]

Such healing must be an ongoing process of continually meeting the triune God's love in prayerful communion at the center or core of our being, discovered in the True Being–God Trinity. What has developed over so many years of self-centered living—as though the world revolved around ourselves—cannot be healed in one moment. It is only God's love, experienced as unconditional, outpoured self-giving through Jesus Christ in his Spirit, the divine uncreated energies touching us in the context of our daily, historical experiences and calling us into divine filiation of our true self in his divine Sonship, that alone truly heals.

THE TRANSFORMATION OF THE HEART

Dürckheim gives us three stages that develop this process of our heart-transformation into a oneness with Christ, offering us the possibility to discover also in ever increasing awareness of our "otherness," our unique true selfhood in that very oneness with the Word made flesh.

1. All that is contrary to essential being must be relinquished.
2. That which has been relinquished must be dissolved in the Ground of Being which absorbs, redeems, transforms and recreates.
3. The newly formed core arises out of the Ground of Being must be recognized, accepted, allowed to grow and personal responsibility for it undertaken.

We have already developed the first stage, namely, relinquishing the brokenness and negativity of the false self within us. Now we turn to stage two by examining how to pray in the heart—where we experience the personalized Ground of Being as the core and center of our essential self in transcendent prayer. This becomes the state of our experiencing the transformation and recreating of our true self.

HEALING PRAYER-EXERCISE

Here are some steps that you can take to enter into a prayerful inner healing of body, soul and spirit.

• Select a quiet place, free from noise and interruptions. The best time is in early morning before the activities of the day, before sleep in the evening, or if you should wake in the middle of the night.

• Choose a position that is comfortable, yet disciplined enough to prevent sleep or undue distractions to arise. This can be sitting on a cushion on the floor or on a straight chair.

• Localize yourself in the presence of the Trinity by making acts of faith, adoration, hope, and love.

• Begin to breathe consciously. Feel your breath entering into your lungs and slowly follow its exhalation. Synchronized your inhalation and exhalation with the opposite movement of your diaphragm. Lengthen your breathing into calm, long breaths. Feel yourself literally relaxing.

• Consciously start from the head and go through all parts of the body, commanding each part to give up any tension and replacing it with complete relaxation. Enjoy the feeling of become physically whole.

• Descend, by any technique that is meaningful and yields the best results, into the depths of your *heart*, the deeper layers of your consciousness beyond words and images where you are meeting God, as the Ground of Being.

• The most important part of this healing exercise consists in the deep faith that you exercise in the presence of Jesus Christ, the Divine Physician, who is still healing anyone broken, who calls out to him in faith, trust, and love. "I tell you therefore: everything you ask and pray for, believe that you have it already, and it will be yours" (Mk 10:24).

• The first element in such healing, be it on the physical, psychic, or spiritual level, consists in having a forgiving heart toward others who may have injured or hurt you in any way. Feel a oneness as the love of God's Spirit unites you with that person or persons in forgiving love.

• The important and final step in such meditation for healing is this: Picture Jesus from the depths of your heart touching that area of your body, soul, or spirit that needs healing. This may concern a relationship with a person not present. See yourself already healed and living in a new-found joyful love toward that person and all others. Begin to thank God for such a healing. Know it is already being done as you believe.

• Leave such a meditation with a spirit of humble thanksgiving, knowing that God has truly answered your prayer. You are healed! Thank God all that day for such a healing. Act on the conviction that God has heard your prayer and is progressively healing you, even if there is not instant manifestation.

If at the end of this chapter you do not feel moved to seek a concrete healing on a body or psychic or spirit level, perhaps you would prefer to place yourself reverently in the presence of Jesus as your Divine Physician and allow the images of the following poetic meditation to open you up in a childlike trust to his continued healing power.

BROKEN BUT LOVED

I join the crowd of broken people,
hobbling, falling, screaming and crying
in their sickness and inner misery.
Frantically we search, now here, now there.

Can no one heal, us, bring us new life?
We hang on each other and we pull each other down
into a sharing misery added to each other's.

What darkness covers my soul?
What bonds hold me imprisoned!
What leprous wounds cover me
and eat my substance away!

O Jesus, Divine Physician, come
and stretch your healing hands upon me.
Break loose my bonds and set me free.
Dispel the darkness by the Light of your presence.
Thaw the freezing in all my limbs.
Warm my cold isolation with your love.

O most gentle, merciful Savior,
bend over me again and enspirit
these dry bones of mine
with your Spirit that alone brings new life.
Let me feel once more your healing touch,
that resurrects me from the dead,
that quiets the storm within my breast.
Let your love sear through me
like an arrow plunged deep down
into the last resistance in my heart.

Lord and Master, how great is your love,
how ever abiding and everlasting
and, yet, how blinded I was to your great Light,
how absent to your surrendering presence!

I cry out, Savior, that you offer again
that healing love that destroys all sin,

that breaks down prison walls of pride
and sends me forth in humble service
to share your healing love with others.

"Here is my love offered to you,
a love of pain, of suffering unto death,
Take and receive my gift of self,
my healing stillness that drives
from your heart all noise and clamor,
my whispering love that shouts to you
of love divine, pursuing, ever present.

This healing love I give to you.
Kneel down to receive this anointing
as kings of old, as consecrated priests,
I send you forth, healed and whole
to be a healing touch of love
to all you meet.
You were broken, but always loved.

Now be love to those who still know
not of my healing, loving power.
Tell them the Good News
that darkness can be turned into Light,
that loneliness can embrace and be united
into a loving community of many
in the oneness of my Love."

Absence is driven out by presence,
brokenness can be healed by Love!

G.A.M.

8

Praying in the Heart

One of the great graces in my life has been my own immersion in the teachings of the early Eastern Christian mystics of the desert and to a limited degree to experience in my own life the dynamic they experienced so profoundly: namely, that weeping and mourning for our brokenness brings us in the littleness of our heart before the all-loving and merciful Trinity and there to receive their healing comfort.

In the West when we speak of compunction, purification, and the constant thought of our sins, we regard it as totally negative. I believe this is precisely because we have lost the concept of our littleness of heart, the conviction resulting from the realization of our true, ontological position in regard to God. It is evident throughout all the Eastern Christian Fathers' writings that the first step in the spiritual life is always to put ourselves before God as we really are, which is in a state of nothingness. We are nothingness before *Allness*, and so it is only natural that we find that Christian spirituality is based on this polarity: the transcendence of God and our own littleness.

But strangely enough, far from breeding in us any sadness or long-faced remorse or introspection, the realization of our nothingness before God is what gives us true Christian joy. Indeed, it fills us with great, childlike confidence in God.

WEEP—THERE IS NO OTHER WAY

This inner weeping for our existential state of "zeroness" is what the Fathers of the East called *penthos* in Greek. It is a permanent environment wherein a true relationship with God is maintained. This is the only way that God will reveal himself to us. All that we can learn on our own about God is really nothing or so very little, but when God reveals himself to us, and he does this only to the meek and humble of heart, then we can make genuine progress in the spiritual life.

Abbot Pimen, one of the early Egyptian Fathers of the desert, expressed the common thinking of the Desert Fathers and Mothers when he said: "Weep for your sins, there is no other way to salvation." They were completely convinced that such weeping kept them from sinning and that this was the only way to true salvation, to true life, whereby God, even in this life, would come and dwell within them in their hearts.

THE BIRTH OF TRUE PRAYER

True, fiery prayer rises up from the depths of our hearts as a fruit of repentance and a continued conversion. The heart opens up and is poured out in deep yearning for oneness in loving unity with the indwelling Trinity. This we can call, in the words of the Eastern Fathers, the *prayer of the heart.*

Such prayer of the heart bursts out from the depths of our heartfelt distress with our wretchedness, as St. Paul expressed: "What a wretched man I am! Who will rescue me from this body doomed to death? Thanks be to God through Jesus Christ our Lord!" (Rm 7:24–25).

Inner joyful sweetness will gradually dominate in our hearts as we experience the depths of our won sinfulness and brokenness by plunging into the depths of God's tender mercy. God in his great mercy granted to the sinful woman in the Gospel (Lk 7:47) forgiveness of her sins and a deep union with him "for she loved much." God loves those who love him. He cleaves to those who cleave to him. He gives himself to those who ardently seek him unceasingly. He abundantly grants fullness of joy to those who desire to enjoy his love.

St. Theophan the Recluse gives us a beginning description of the prayer of the heart as taught by all the Desert Fathers:

> To kindle in his heart such a divine love, to unite with God in an inseparable union of love, it is necessary for a man to pray often, raising the mind to God. For as a flame increases when it is constantly fed, so prayer, made often, with the mind dwelling ever more deeply in God, arouses divine love in the heart. And the heart, set on fire, will warm all the inner man, will enlighten and teach him, revealing to him all its unknown and hidden wisdom, and making him like a flaming Seraph, always standing before God within his spirit, always looking at him within his mind, and drawing from this vision the sweetness of spiritual joy.[1]

FIERY PRAYER

It was Cassian who spoke the language of the hesychastic (those who pray in the depths of their hearts) Fathers of the desert in describing such wordless contemplation as "fiery prayer":

> We are affected from the very bottom of our heart, so that we get at its meaning (Holy Scripture), not by reading the text, but by experience anticipating its meaning. And so our soul will arrive at that purity of prayer reached, to the extent that the Lord permit it. . . . This is masked by no attendant sounds of words. It is a *fiery* outbreak, an indescribable exaltation, an insatiable thrust of the soul. Free of what is sensed and seen, ineffable in its groans and signs, the soul pours itself out to God.[2]

It is God who has put this yearning to be set on fire by the ever-new levels of union with God that we, by God's grace through his condescending love and mercy, can attain. We burn within our hearts to become more one with God. "God, you are my God, I am seeking you, my soul is thirsting for you, my flesh is longing for you, a land parched, weary and waterless; I long to gaze on you in the Sanctuary" (Ps 63:1–2).

No life is worth living without living in oneness with God within our hearts. Yet to attain this requires a dying process as we allow God to strip from us all that prevents us from surrendering ourselves completely to his love. Tired of fleeing from God's mercy, in the words of the poet Francis Thompson, we reach the point of true conversion to stand naked before God and allow him to hack from us every binding force that keeps us from surrendering at every moment to God's infinite love:

Naked I wait Thy love's uplifted stroke!
My harness piece by piece Thou hast hewn from me,
And smitten to my knee;
I am defenceless utterly. . . .

"All which I took from thee I did but take,
Not for thy harms,
But just that thou might'st seek it in My arms.
All of which thy child's MISTAKE
Fancies as lost, I have stored for thee at home. . . .
Ah, fondest, blindest, weakest,
I am He Whom thou seekest!
Thou dravest love from thee, who dravest Me."[3]

STRETCHING OUT TOWARD GOD

Our wounds are dressed and healed by God's sweet balm of merciful love. Our only response is to give continued glory to God for his marvels of merciful love. Our only response is to give continued glory to God for his marvels of love and mercy. Now our deepest yearnings of the heart become the path to heaven. The distance from our heart into the heart of God is measured, not by miles, but by the constancy and intensity of our returned love and our continued desire to surrender totally to God.

With St. Paul we can say: "All I can say is that I forget the past and I strain ahead for what is still to come. I am racing for the finish,. for the prize to which God calls up upwards to receive in Christ Jesus" (Ph 3:14–15). But to forget the past and to stretch forth into the next moment to possess God more completely in our hearts, we must learn to live continually in God's presence.

Jesus still tells us as he spoke to the hearts of the desert ascetics of the early Church that all Christians are to pray continually: "Then Jesus told them a parable about the need to pray continually and never lose heart" (Lk 18:1). Jesus taught his disciples: "Watch you, therefore, and pray always" (Lk 21:36, KJV).

St. Paul challenged the early Christians in Thessalonica to pray continually:

Be happy at all times; pray constantly; and for all things give thanks to God, because this is what God expects you to do in Christ Jesus. (1 Thes 5:17–18)

TO PRAY ALWAYS

Is it possible for us modern men and women, living in a world of so much movement, noise, pollution of air and waterways, crime, and cities of decaying garbage heaps and toxic wastes, to find the inner peace to maintain a "recollection" in our hearts of the indwelling presence that would allow us to pray always? From earliest times in Christianity, people sought an expanded consciousness of God's abiding presence within them, in their *hearts*.

They reached out for an ever-increasing awareness, constancy, and sincerity in their intimate relationships with the
indwelling Father, Son, and Holy Spirit. The hermits that fled
into the stark, barren deserts were seeking an expansion of
consciousness that God was truly the Source and absolute
Spirit that drove them into the desert, primarily of their hearts,
to love God with their whole heart, their whole soul, mind, and
strength. The heart, as we have already pointed out, represents
in Scripture in the language of all mystics the deepest part of
the whole, integrated person. St. Theophan the Recluse expressed this early inner attention as a focusing in the heart
upon God in reverent fear and hope:

> Prayer is turning the mind and thoughts towards God. To pray
> means to stand before God with the mind, mentally to gaze
> unswervingly at him, to converse with him in reverent fear and
> hope. . . . The principal thing is to stand with the mind in the
> heart before God, and to go on standing before him unceasingly
> day and night, until the end of life. . . . Behave as you wish, so
> long as you learn to stand before God with the mind in the heart,
> for in this lies the essence of the matter.[4]

Such early Christians did not believe that the injunctions of
Jesus to stand vigilantly attentive in the heart and pray incessantly were to be interpreted as Semitic hyperbole. They believed the great truth Jesus came to reveal to us and made possible through the infused power of the Spirit of his gifts of
faith, hope, and love, exercised at every moment in every
thought, word, and deed—namely, that the Trinity, the Father,
Son, and Holy Spirit, truly lived within them. The result for all
Christians was to become more and more aware daily of that
greatest of all realities.

For such heroically dedicated Christians, prayer was more
than saying fixed prayers or asking God for gifts and even
thanking him for gifts received. Prayer was a state of being, of
living beyond the habitual idea that they had of themselves or

that their society fashioned for them. It was a continued journey within, a return to their true selves, by living as consciously as possible in loving surrender to God as their Source and their final goal.

The means to attain such prayer of the heart, they knew, would be all the practices of asceticism of fasting, vigils, hard physical work, guarding the heart against the eight capital vices by putting on the mind and virtues of Jesus Christ. Yet they humbly knew that whatever efforts they used to gain the inner purity of heart, it would not lie in their power to reach this state of "pure" prayer by such efforts alone.

It was the work of the Holy Spirit who prayed in us (Rm 8:26–26) with our spirit, our heart, by pouring into our emptied hearts the gifts of faith, hope, and love to surrender in all anxieties through childlike trust to the constant love of the heavenly Father and to grace us with humble love toward our neighbors. St. Paul clearly teaches this:

> These are the very things that God has revealed to us through the Spirit, for the Spirit reaches the depths of everything, even the depths of God. After all, the depths of a man can only be known by the Spirit of God. Now instead of the spirit of the world, we have received the Spirit that comes from God, to teach us to understand the gifts that he has given us. . . . A spiritual man, on the other hand, is able to judge the value of everything, and his own value is not to be judged by other men. . . . But we are those who have the mind of Christ. (1 Cor 2:10–16)

REMEMBERING GOD'S PRESENCE

Praying in the heart did not bring with it a special esoteric technique of *gnosis* given to only the initiated. It is basically an effective attitude that seeks to transcend the limitations of human words and mental images to reach an inner "still point" where God and the individual Christian meet in silent self-surrendering love.

In the third century Origen taught that one's daily works and the keeping of the divine commandments should never take a Christian away from true prayer. All the Fathers taught that true prayer does not mean complete concentration with all one's strength upon God. For Origen, to pray without ceasing was to combine prayer with one's necessary works. A Christian's prayerfulness would be determined by the degree to which one's action and inner prayerful attitude came from the love of God.[5]

It was St. Basil in his prudence that brought constant prayer into the practical dimension of ordinary persons living in the world. He knew it was not practical for most monks ever, let alone the average lay person. to recite continually, orally or mentally, a fixed ejaculation or aspiration as a way of centering upon God always. He has bequeathed to all succeeding generations the phrase, "to attend to yourself," to refer to an inner attentiveness or a state of alert consciousness of God's ever-abiding presence and an active desire on the part of the individual Christian to live in harmony with God's holy will, manifested at every moment, but especially in the concreteness of *this* very moment and in the context of this or that action or rest. St. Basil describes this inner state of attentiveness to do all for God's glory:

> We should watch over our heart with all vigilance, not only to avoid ever losing the thought of God or sullying the memory of his wonders by vain imaginations, but also in order to carry about the holy thoughts of God stamped upon our souls as an ineffaceable seal by continuous and pure recollection . . . as the Christian directs every action, small and great, according to the will of God, performing the action at the same time with care and exactitude, and keeping his thoughts fixed upon the One who gave him the work to do . . . . We should perform every action as if under the eyes of the Lord and think every thought as if observed by him . . . fulfilling the words of the Lord: "I seek not my own will but the will of him that sent me, the Father."[6]

Thus we see that if a person does not have this desire to direct all thoughts, words, and deeds unto God's glory by remembering God's loving presence, then even the constant recitation of prayers and the performance of heroic works will not be pleasing to God. It is such remembrance of God, the indwelling Trinity, that allows us Christians to direct all of our thought, words, and deeds toward God.

THE JESUS PRAYER

The Fathers of the desert were not running from cities or from human civilization, but they were running into their deepest selves to find themselves on a higher level of existence—as Jesus Christ, the risen Lord, who dwelt within them, became the focal center of their true selves in him. They strove to live constantly in the consciousness of God's loving presence and to surrender themselves completely to his holy will.

When the Fathers urge us to such a prayer of the heart, they suggest the simple but powerful "Jesus Prayer." They had learned to enter into the deepest areas of their unconscious, and there they found the demonic within themselves. They knew from their Christian faith and experience that there was no other name whereby they would be saved and healed than the name of Jesus (Acts 4:11).

In the Christian East, the Christian learned to synchronize one's breathing with the invocation of the sacred name of Jesus. With no discursive thought about the content of the prayer, the Eastern Christians learned to occupy their senses and imagination with a fixed point of attention that then freed their mind to be docile and supple to God operating in a nonverbal manner.[7]

THE NAME OF JESUS

By understanding the psychology of the Semite who believed the person named to be present to the one pronouncing the name with reverence and love, we can better appreciate, not only the Christians' reverence and love for the name of Jesus, but also their insight into the presence of the risen Savior by pronouncing that name. This understanding could open to us today a great source of biblical spirituality and a form of simple, relaxed prayer that could be most helpful for all of us in our everyday dash-about world.

The "Jesus Prayer," which eventually over the years took on a fixed formula: "Lord, Jesus Christ, Son of God, have mercy on me, a sinner," has its roots not only in the New testament, but even farther back in the Old Testament. In the Old Covenant we see a developed personal conviction that the invocation of the name of God brought with it the conscious realization of his presence: "Call on my Name, I will hear" (Zec 13:9).

But the New Testament gives us a fuller theology of God's name and the power that emanates from the reverent pronouncing of the name of Jesus.

St. Paul tells us that "God has given him a name that is above all names in that at the name of Jesus every knee shall bend in heaven, on earth and under the earth" (Ph 2:9–10). The Acts of the Apostles describe how the good news is preached in the name of Jesus. Converts believe Jesus is truly the Son of God. Christians encounter him in the sacraments that are administered in his sacred name. Miracles are wrought by uttering his name. Martyrs die, pronouncing it reverently.

There is no tone of magic—only a deep conviction among the early Christians that Jesus Christ, true God and true man, who died and was raised up by his heavenly Father, still lived within them and was leading them to a share in his resurrected life. The Gospel stories of the two blind men on the road crying, "Son of David, have mercy on us" (Mt 9:27), and the humble request of the publican, "O God, have mercy on me, a sinner" (Lk 18:13), became the inspiration for this prayer.

Whether a Christian used the entire, traditional formula: "Lord, Jesus Christ, Son of God, have mercy on me, a sinner" or merely the name of "Jesus—mercy," what is important in praying the name and person of Jesus in our heart is to enter into the dynamics of true heart-prayer.

This includes three dynamic, interpersonal relationships between the Christian and the risen Lord Jesus: the *transcendence* of Jesus as Son of God, truly divine, of the same nature as the Father; the humble sense of our individual brokenness, *sinfulness*, and inability to heal ourselves; and lastly, the intimate experience of the *immanence* of the indwelling Trinity within the Christian, who continuously experiences his/her uniqueness in the Trinity's healing love.

A TRUE RELIGIOUS EXPERIENCE

Any true Christian religious experience must first place a strong accent on the awesomeness and complete *transcendence* of Jesus Christ. He is Lord, He is the Creator and Redeemer of us all. He is more than just a good man, more even than a Superstar. He is God! "Lord, Jesus Christ, Son of God!" We must first recognize this awesome fact.

Second, we must recognize that we are sinners. St. James tells us to humble ourselves before God by realizing our sinfulness: "Realize that you have been disloyal and get your hearts made true once more. As you come close to God you should be deeply sorry, you should be grieved, you should even be in tears—you will have to feel very small in the sight of God before he will set you on your feet once more" (Js 4:7–10).

Third, what binds us sinners to Jesus, the Lord and God Almighty, is our hunger for his presence with us and within us, "more intimately to me than I to myself," as Augustine wrote, Paul tells us:" He is not far from any of us. Indeed, it is in him that we live and move and have our being" (Acts 17:28). Because Jesus Christ is Lord and God, completely perfect and transcendent to all creatures, he is able also to be the ground of our being, living within us, sustaining us in being. "All creation took place through him, and none took place without him" (Jn 1:3).

St. Peter typified these three characteristics of a religious experience. When Jesus told Peter and his companions to lower their nets to a miraculous catch of fish, Peter, overwhelmed by Jesus' power, threw himself at his feet and said, "Depart from me, Lord, for I am a sinful man" (Lk 5:8). He was awed by the transcendence of Jesus as the Son of God, and along with that he sensed his own unworthiness before the greatness of Jesus the Lord; finally he showed a desire to hold fast to him as he clung to his feet in adoring worship: "Lord Jesus Christ, Son of God, have mercy on me, a sinner."

OUR TRUE SELF IN JESUS

The Eastern spiritual writers would say that, as we are faithful to the simple, heartfelt encounter with Jesus in our heart through the repetition of his holy name, we will gradually experience his presence deep down within our true person at the core of our very being. As God lives in the depths of our being, he will no longer be a mere concept to us, but a living person, penetrating us deeply. We will become more and more what God created us to be, the image of his own divine Son. We will become aware of our true self, not as a subject adoring some being who dwells in the remoteness of heaven, but as a child of God, participating, as St. Peter says, in the divine nature (2 Pt 1:4). We will not become God by nature, but will truly be made Godlike by God's presence within.

THE RELEASE OF THE HOLY SPIRIT

The Eastern authors would also say that the presence of Jesus brought vividly to our consciousness by the reverent pronouncing of his Sacred Name, above all, releases the Holy Spirit within us. And the Spirit of Jesus reveals all we need to know about our personal Savior (Jn 15: 26), the Divine Lord. Above all, the Spirit of Love gives us the power to know that we are loved in all circumstances of life by a tender, loving Father. The Holy Spirit of Jesus speaks to us deeply within our hearts and tells us that we really are God's children (Rom 8:16). We can now rightly speak of God as our dear Father, *Abba* (Gal 4:6).

A WAY OF LIFE

The "Jesus Prayer" is, in the final analysis, a way of life "in Christ Jesus," a phrase that St. Paul never tires of using. This living person dwells within us, giving us his Spirit and his power to love the Father with his own love and to love one another as he loves us. When we call upon his name incessantly, Jesus the Lord continually reveals to us the Father. Jesus is always saying; "And I have revealed you [Father] to them and I will keep on revealing you so that the mighty love you have for me may be in them and I in them" (Jn 17:26).

In leading us to the Father, Jesus brings us into a total presence of the Trinity where we experience the three distinct persons, Father, Son, and Holy Spirit, as uncreated energies of love, each giving himself to us in the imaged self-emptying Son of God, dying on the cross for love of each of us. Sun's rays can flash off a prism and give colored light. The same rays can hit a lens and become concentrated fire. Not only do they illuminate, but they burn with the heat of fire.

This is similar to the experience of the continuous repetition, in loving adoration of the name of Jesus. The presence of Jesus generates a burning love within our hearts. A unity that simplifies the whole mystery of God's infinite love in the first creation, the incarnation, redemption, and our sanctification, takes over and operates in our hearts. Christ, in Paul's words, lives in your hearts through faith; and, then, planted in love and built on love, you will with all the saints have strength to grasp the breadth and the length, the height and the depth; until, knowing the love of Christ, which is beyond all knowledge, you are filled with the utter fullness of God. (Eph 3:17–19)

Synchronizing this name and person with our breath, we know by experience that he is our very breath, our very life. Our "magnificent obsession" becomes the consciousness of his increasing and our proportionate decreasing before his allness. Only the Holy Spirit can lead us into that intimate, mysterious knowledge which Paul wanted to possess: "All I want is to know Christ and the power of his resurrection and to share his sufferings by reproducing the pattern of his death" (Ph 3:10).

PRAYER OF THE HEART AND TECHNIQUES

There are many levels of application to our spiritual life in our modern times of the spirituality of the prayer of the heart as taught and practiced by the early desert mystics. The first and most primary benefit to be received from such a spirituality is that you and I retain in our heart the constant stretching forth in the fullness of our freedom as children of God in our desire pray incessantly by living in the presence of the indwelling Trinity within our heart, as the core of our being. The meaning of our Christian life is not to repeat a Christian mantra over and over, but to seek to attain ever more that full meaning of our human existence—to move at all times into greater awareness of God's intimate and immediate loving presence, which is to be discovered or unveiled in each moment.

We can attain this through our inner discipline to uproot any pride and self-centeredness, and to put on the mind of Christ by striving for purity of heart. We do this by accepting the triune God as uncreated energies of love, always actively drawing us as primary grace to share in the Trinity's image and likeness.

To live in the presence of the risen Lord Jesus who is continually releasing his Spirit, who leads us to the Father, we may be drawn to focus on Jesus as our inner Savior, risen and raising us to eternal life by means of the "Jesus Prayer." The Fathers of the desert show a wonderful freedom of selecting the "name" of Jesus. What is important is not any given formula, as if the words making up the prayer are capable of producing a magical effect. The Spirit reveals in you how that name and presence of Jesus will best come to you in the "incarnation" of a breath prayer.

Any technique used in prayer is only a means to greater union with Christ, the Way to the Father through the Holy Spirit. The German theologian Johannes Lotz lays down for us a prudent guideline in the use of any word-prayer to aid us in greater presence to the indwelling presence:

> Methods should never be allowed to do violence to our individuality, but they should be used to free it and adapt it for the work of meditation so that each meditator can find his own way.[8]

Prayer of the heart is the gift of contemplation without words or images that come under our own choosing or discursive control and is always the gratuitous infusion by the Holy Spirit—it is never dependent on our efforts. Yet a focus of integrating body, soul, and spirit levels on the name and inner presence of Jesus Christ, Son of God, has been a great aid in praying more deeply within the heart by thousands and thousands of Christians down through the ages.

DISCOVERING OUR TRUE SELF
IN CHRIST IN OUR HEART

What we have been presenting in this chapter on praying in our heart is a form of contemplative prayer where God's Spirit gives us a new presence of the Trinity dwelling within us, but that is revealed as a "luminous darkness" in St. Gregory of Nyssa's words. It is a true experience in God-given knowledge of the length, breadth, width, and depth of the knowledge of Jesus Christ that surpasses all other human understanding (Eph 3:18). This is given us as we bring our mind, our habitual level of consciousness, into our "heart," that inner cave that is fashioned as a spiritual womb by the uncreated energies of God's love, the Holy Spirit, and in deep, dark, stark faith, we cry out: "Lord, Jesus Christ, have mercy on us sinners!" and surrender totally in renewed freedom to turn our lives over to God's complete domination.

This is the *apophatic* knowledge that only the Holy Spirit can infuse into our consciousness, a true knowing by unknowing. Pseudo-Dionysius of the fifth century expressed this unanimous teaching of the Fathers of the desert that gives us the essence of the prayer of the heart:

> And then it [God's essence in darkness] breaks forth, even from the things that are beheld and from those that behold them, and plunges the true initiate into the darkness of unknowing wherein he renounces all the apprehensions of his understanding and is enwrapped in that which is wholly intangible and invisible, belonging wholly to him that is beyond all things and to none else (whether himself or another), and being through the passive stillness of all his reasoning powers united by his highest faculty to him that is wholly unknowable, of whom thus by a rejection of all knowledge he possesses a knowledge that exceeds his understanding.[9]

The prayer of the heart is the Eastern Christian's way of describing the ongoing process of a human being returning to his or her true state, to a consciousness of uniqueness by *being* in Christ.[10]

Through the love received through the Spirit that lives within the divinized human "heart" or consciousness (Rm 5:5), the Christian seeks at all times to live according to that inner dignity ever experienced within the heart in all human relationships and daily events. The prayer of the heart and its authenticity must be measured, as Jesus insisted upon in the Gospels, by the fruit produced in our lives.

We live out our Baptism, as we cry out to Jesus to release his Spirit of love within our hearts. Through a dynamic process of ongoing purifications and deaths to selfishness, we rise to a more intense, conscious relationship to God. We attain a state of inner harmony and peace, tranquillity and resting in God as our true Center. There is peace and joy in the oneness attained with the indwelling Trinity. There is also a burning desire to possess still more the "absent" God by stretching out in a willed desire to surrender ourselves more completely, to suffer even more for love of God and neighbor.

PRAYER-EXERCISE

1. Using the simple techniques previously outlined, integrate, through your diaphragmatic breathing deeply in and out, your body and soul and spirit levels. Feel yourself completely relaxing. Enter into the spirit-level in your "heart" through faith that the Holy Spirit is praying with your "spirit" within your deepest consciousness, permeated by the Spirit's faith, hope, and love.

2. As you slowly breathe in, think: "Lord Jesus Christ." As you slowly breathe out, think: "Son of God."

3. Breathe in again and think: "Have mercy." Breathe out and think: "On me a sinner."

4. Repeat, striving to lengthen your breathing as you gently slip into a deeper state of relaxation, while moving yourself to greater self-surrender to me indwelling Trinity. Gently move beyond any confining words into the presence of the Father, Son, and Spirit. Become one with Divinity within you! Yet discover your uniqueness, your true giftedness from the uncreated energies of the Father, Son, and Spirit, now capable of

more consciously surrendering your entire being to the in-dwelling Trinity.

If you feel yourself "touching" God and God permeating you, let go of the words. You can gently come back to your rhythmic breathing as you synchronize the words of the prayer with your breathing if you find yourself becoming diffused and distracted away from Center.

5. Try this formula for several days, going no longer than twenty minutes at one sitting. During the day, while at your busy occupations, find time to turn within and briefly syn-chronize your breathing the "Jesus Prayer" of a shortened form, such as: "Jesus—Mercy!"

9

The Heart of Christ

In the powerful play about Helen Keller there is a climactic scene that heralds a breakthrough in communication between her faithful teacher, Annie Sullivan, and the child ,Helen. Over and over with immense patience, the teacher had signed the simple word "water" in the hand of the child. But one day she signed it and placed Helen's hand under the outdoor water pump's spout. As the water flowed over her hand, a new world named "water" and a human person, Helen, were born as the communicating word from out of God's mind leapt from the child's hand to her mind and then out to a new world of reality. God's reality—through a single word.

St. Augustine defined a human being as one who is *capax Dei*—capable of knowing and loving God. But we have been made for this potentiality only because we are also *capax mundi*, capable of receiving God's communication in knowledge and love, in and through the Word of God in whom the world around us has its being.

GOD'S WORD IN CREATION

If God's essence is love, as Judaeo-Christianity reveals to us, then he is always seeking to share his being by communicating his presence to us, whom he creates according to his image and likeness (Gn 1:26–27) through his Word. God becomes a God-toward-others by communicating himself in the gifts of creation through his Word and his Spirit of love. The entire world around us is being created in an ongoing process of God's symbol of his burning desire to give himself in faithful communication to us through his Word.

The world at its interior is filled with the self-communicating Trinity. God is filling the universe with his loving Self. His uncreated energies swirl through and fill all creatures with his loving, creative presence. "Yahweh's love fills the earth. By the word of Yahweh the heavens were made, their whole array by the breath of his mouth" (Ps 33:5–6).

Not only does God communicate himself in creation, but he is sustaining, directing God. He evolves his presence that is locked into his creation through his Word that is continually being communicated over millions of years. Not one of us human beings can complain that God has never spoken his word to him or her. St. Paul clearly shows the universality to all human beings of God's revelation of himself in all of creation:

> For what can be known about God is perfectly plain to them since God himself has made it plain. Ever since God created the world his everlasting power and deity—however invisible–have been there for the mind to see in the things he has made. That is why such people are without excuse: they knew God and yet refused to honor him as God or to thank him; instead, they made nonsense out of logic and their empty minds were darkened. (Rm 1:19–21)

AND THE WORD BECAME FLESH

John in his Gospel *Prologue* establishes a breathtaking perspective that covers the whole universe that ever was, is, or ever will be. It is in the presence of the perfect possessor of all being that we watch the created world slowly begin to move under the dynamic power of God's Word from the coldness of nothingness into the warmth of being. It is the Word that brings the universe from its existence in the mind of God into actual existence. It is not a static role that began and is now finished. Whatever created beings are coming into existence or moving to a greater degree of existence, there the *Logos* is operative. For there can be no progression in being except through the Logos who is the source of all being.

And then John wrote the words that constitute the Good News of how great is God's love for us:

> And the Word became flesh
> and made his dwelling among us,
> and we saw his glory,
> the glory as of the Father's only Son,
> full of grace and truth. (Jn 1:14)

John is telling us that the progressive dwelling of God in his powerful glory in all of creation and in the tent of the meeting among his chosen people and in Solomon's temple and in his prophets is now fully present. He fully communicates the invisible God to human beings who accept this Word-made-flesh, Jesus Christ. Everything Jesus Christ now says or does is the Word of God. God no longer needs to speak through his prophets (Heb 1:1–2). Jesus speaks God's complete presence to his people. Whether he touches a leper and heals him or claims absolute authority to forgive sins, Jesus is God communicating his Word to us human beings. His action, as Bultmann says, is a speaking: whatever he says is action.[1]

GOD NOW HAS A HEART

The incredible good news is that in Jesus Christ, the Word of God made flesh, God is human. He is one just like you and me! He has taken on our "flesh." He is a whole person, an embodied being, an ensouled being, an inspirited being. Now God has a human heart! God has a human center and enjoys the freedom all of us have, not merely to avoid evil and do good, but to take his divine-human life and to return it completely in total self-surrender back to his Father.

In this chapter we can now more perfectly understand what the human heart means by understanding what the heart of Christ means. We will understand what it means, then, to be made "according to the image and likeness of God" (Gn 1:26). We will better understand the true purpose of our life by discovering in the context of our daily existence on this earth how we can find our unique and true self in the "heart" of Jesus Christ. Thus we can fulfill in an ever-increasing awareness through faith, hope, and love of the Spirit the great commandments of God brought together in a unity-with-difference: to love God with our whole heart and to love our neighbor as we love ourselves.

Thus it was important in this book to have first explored what our human heart means in terms of what basic cultures throughout all of human history and the main religions and, above all, what the Old and New Testaments have described *heart* to be. This has made it possible now to talk about the universal understanding of the symbol of heart to symbolize ourselves living at the core or center of our being. In our deepest self we begin to live in transcendence or complete openness and receptivity to the mystery of God's revelation in continued conversion away from our hardened heart of selfishness and pride. We find healing and newness of life that sends us forth in "mission" as living and active members of the Body of Christ in humble service to our neighbors.

UNDERSTANDING PRIMORDIAL SYMBOLS

We can apply the symbol of heart to the heart of Christ as God's primordial Logos or Word from all eternity, enfleshed in the unity-in-difference, the Word made flesh, divinity and humanity in the one person of Jesus Christ. He makes it possible for us to understand how his physical heart, which was pierced on the cross and emptied out completely for love of us human beings (Jn 19:34), becomes the physico-psychic symbol of divine and human love totally poured out for love of each of us individual human beings. As the divine Logos made flesh, Jesus shows us how to love God with our whole heart as he does. He shows us how to love our neighbor as he loves us as his neighbors with his human heart.

Karl Rahner, one of the most prolific Catholic writers of theology of our century, provides us with a linguistic analysis of what a symbol is. In his theology of symbols, he applies the symbol of heart to a solid Christology and Trinitarian theology. He critiques the popular devotion to the Sacred Heart and offers us some guidelines to recapture and enliven for our modern times the traditional and essential elements of devotion to the heart of Christ. He does this by purifying the Sacred Heart devotion form elements that have encrusted it with outdated piety and practices no longer viable for Christianity in the modern world.

PRIMORDIAL WORD (*URWORTE*)

Rahner distinguishes between "primary" words and "utility" words. We human beings are by nature "symbolic—we speak words that are symbols that not only signify what we mean to communicate in speech or other concrete, material uses of symbols, but effect an entrance into the mystery of who we are and what we wish to become through such a communication.

"Utility" words are words that we invent to name things, as did Adam in the Garden of Eden (Gn 3:19). We name the things we experience in our relationships with the material world around us. Such words have usually only one meaning, are univocal, and their meaning is exhausted by the thing they define.[2]

"Primordial" words, however, by their intrinsic nature, name a reality that can never be exhausted by a definition that "defines" conceptually the nature of the signified. According to Rahner, such primordial words express things or relationships that are universal and are not limited by cultural or technological development. Such words usually evoke subjective reactions from the human person. Primordial words name objective realities but are never limited to such objective realities. Within the context of subjective reactions and objectivity, a fundamental unity is never lost. Finally, and most important, the person naming a reality with a primordial word not only experiences the dynamic between the unity and multiplicity captured in the reality so named, but the individual person also experiences within her/himself a basic unity through the multiplicity of the created world other than what the subject is. Primordial words give birth to an unlimited sense of a rich mystery that unfolds in the dialectic of "unity-in-difference," to use Rahner's oft-repeated phrase.[3]

THE PRIMORDIAL WORD: HEART

Rahner defines symbol as that "in which one reality renders another present (primarily 'for itself' and only secondarily for others) . . . the representation which allows the other 'to be there.' "[4] A symbol and what it symbolizes are not extrinsic to one another but are intimately and intrinsically related.

When we take the example of the flesh and muscle of the human heart, we see that it leads beyond mere anatomy of the human body: it is a symbol that opens us up to the mystery of the inner center of an individual person. The inner center of a person discovers itself and expresses itself through its bodiliness, in particular, through the kinds of intimate, interior activities associated with the human heart such as longing, choosing, loving, sinning, and surrendering.[5]

A short synthesis of Rahner's understanding of the primordial word "heart" is found in his *Concise Theological Dictionary*:

> HEART. A basic concept of primitive anthropology ("primordial word") which designates that single center of the personal spirit's self-control and psychosomatic autonomy which can only be reached asymptotically. It cannot, of course, be localized in the physical heart, but the latter is its primordial symbol. Strictly speaking, the heart is peculiar to man, being the primordial unity of man who is naturally and substantially composite (at once body and soul). The heart is also the dynamic principle which drives man to seek that ultimate and ultimately unattainable understanding of himself which can only be found in his own heart.[6]

The human heart is the center of one's freedom to make choices in relationship with God, oneself, and others. We can turn within and block out any transcendence to the mystery of being and the discovery in loving relationships to God and neighbor by turning into the darkness of selfishness and pride.

THE HEART OF CHRIST

The symbol of heart involves a double movement. First there is a movement inward in which the "core of the human person" is discovered. The second movement is outward in which the personal center symbolized in the heart related to others and to God. This is seen in Rahner's description of the human heart:

> Heart . . . denotes the core of the human person which is original and inmost with respect to everything else in the human per-

son . . . at which therefore man is originally and wholly related to other persons and above all also to God.[7]

Thus when we speak of the "heart of Christ," we are referring to the human, corporeal heart of Jesus born of Mary. But we cannot separate the symbol of the heart of Christ from what it symbolizes–which is to open us up directly to the inner core of his real person as God-man. It leads us inward to that unique, personal unity that makes him one person in both a divine and a human nature, a unity-in-difference. We must adhere to the dogmatic statement of the Christology of the Council of Chalcedon (451 A.D.), that in Christ there is a distinction but not a separation of the two natures of Christ, with no admixture of assimilation of the human nature into the divine, as the heretical teaching of *monophysitism* held.

But when we speak of the heart of Christ the implications are infinitely more profound. We speak of the "center" of our Lord's human being, which immediately lifts us up into the infinite realm of the very mystery of the divine Trinity. This flows from the fact that the human nature assumed by the Logos, the second person of the Trinity, has its being in the personal unity that is the Son of God in the Trinity.[8]

ACTS ATTRIBUTED TO THE WHOLE PERSON

Thus the thoughts, words, action, and attitudes that flow out of that personal core, symbolized by the physical heart of Christ, are truly the acts and attitudes of the Son of God within the Trinity.[9] Jesus could say: "Whoever has seen me has seen the Father" (Jn 14:9). Whatever flows out of the deepest core of Jesus Christ's being must be attributed to his unique person, the unified person of Jesus Christ. As Rahner points out, such visible acts and attitudes must not be seen as extrinsic to the Logos, since that would mean that the human nature of Christ was either not really appropriated or was swallowed up and not made his own.[10]

We would not be redeemed unless the person, God-man, Jesus Christ, had sacrificed himself out of love for all of us. The symbol of this perfect love of God is for Rahner the pierced human heart of Christ on the cross.[11]

HEART OF CHRIST: SYMBOL OF THE TRINITY

If the physical heart of Jesus Christ symbolizes the inner, personal center of the Logos made man, then the Logos becomes the symbol of the expression in human communication of the God-man, Christ—of the love of the heavenly Father through the Holy Spirit toward all his children. Rahner clearly sees the intrinsic connection between the inner Trinitarian love, the self-emptying love between the Father and the Son through the *kenotic* or emptying love that is called the Holy Spirit, who proceeds from the Father and the Son and binds them into a "unity-in-difference," and the authentic Christian teaching of Christology.

The ineffable mystery of the Trinity that escapes our own human comprehension can, however, be known and experienced in and through Jesus Christ and the Holy Spirit. God not only deemed to reveal the truth of this mystery to us, but in that revelation he has made the mystery of the Trinity the beginning and the end of all reality. God effects our fulfillment precisely in and through the activities of the triune God in the context of our history of salvation.

That is why Rahner posits the very important and fundamental truth of Christianity that has for so long been overlooked by most Western theologians. This oversight is perhaps due mainly to a misunderstanding of how the heart of the God-man not only symbolizes but effects through the hidden, self-emptying, kenotic Holy Spirit the relationships of the loving Trinity toward the created world, especially toward us human beings. This principle is: "The 'economic Trinity' is the 'immanent Trinity' and the 'immanent Trinity' is the 'economic' Trinity."[12]

There must be a connection between the Trinity and ourselves or else the purpose of the incarnation of the Word made flesh would have no intrinsic bearing on Jesus Christ, the imaging of the Father through the Spirit and the possibility of transforming us by that inner Trinitarian life into becoming really "children of God" (1 Jn 3:1). This principle stresses the personalism of the three divine Persons in their one "essential" act of self-communication to human beings. If this were not so, Rahner argues: "God would be the 'giver,' not the gift itself. He would 'give himself' only to the extent that he communicates a gift distinct from himself."[13]

But the Good News is that Jesus makes it possible for us to believe and respond to the power of the risen Lord, his Spirit, that we become divinized children of God, "sharers of God's very own nature" (2 Pt 1:4). God so loves us as a Trinitarian community through his pierced heart on the cross, so does the Father, with the Spirit and the Son-Logos, love us and continually in the context of our daily lives gives himself in and through his "two hands" in the words of St. Irenaeus of the second century, Jesus Christ, and the Holy Spirit.[14]

TRANSFORMING LOVE

Through the heart of Christ, therefore, we come to see that redemption and creation are not static, objective, moments of the past. Each day in prayer, Jesus, the Way, the Truth, and the Life (Jn 14:6), through his Spirit helps us discover afresh that the Father, Son, and Spirit live toward us in serving love. Such love is always the eternal, unchanging, unconditional self-giving of the Father, Son, and Spirit to us in their uncreated energies of love.[15]

Yet such love is ever being unveiled in new and exciting ways. Every human situation can work unto good (Rm 8:28). It can be a symbol of working in self-sacrificing love as revealed through the heart of Christ, still loving us with the love that he revealed through the symbol of his pierced heart.

DEVOTION TO THE SACRED HEART

We have developed the meaning of the heart of Christ, especially as the symbol of the intrinsic, personal gift of the God-man, Jesus Christ, as symbolized by his pierced heart, in relation to the fundamental Christian dogma of Christology and the Trinity. Let us now investigate the popular devotion to the Sacred Heart. We wish to do this in order to bring forth the essential elements of what has been traditional throughout the history of Christianity in all ages and to formulate a true devotion to the heart of Christ. This will give us a more dynamic spirituality of the heart, both of Christ and our hearts as the deepest core of our being where the love, symbolized by the pierced heart of Christ, will transform us into pierced hearts of self-emptying love in humble service to our neighbors.

RELEVANCE OF THE DEVOTION FOR TODAY

Many of us who grew up in the Catholic tradition that existed in our parishes and in religious communities before Vatican II felt "at home," and so comfortable that we never questioned the effectiveness of the popular devotion to the Sacred Heart of Jesus. We must always distinguish between the true elements of genuine piety, which flow out of properly revealed teachings of Christianity, and the actual practice of devotional piety toward such revelation. St. Margaret Mary Alacoque, a Visitandine contemplative at Paray-le-Monial in France in the seventeenth century, did much through her visions to shape Western devotion to the Sacred Heart of Jesus. Her interior vision of the Sacred Heart gives us tangible symbols that we can visualize and associate with our own devotion to the Sacred Heart:

> The divine Heart was represented to me as upon a throne of fire and flames. It shed rays on every side, brighter than the sun and transparent as crystal. The wound which He received on the cross appeared there visibly. A crown of Thorns encircled the divine Heart and it was surmounted by a cross.[16]

We are all familiar with the popular aspects of devotion to the Sacred Heart of Jesus. In our modern culture, as we grow in deeper prayer and are swept up into a new sense of world community, such concrete images and practices of this devotion can become a real obstacle to true devotion to Jesus Christ, who is fully God and fully man. We are all acquainted with the pictures and statues of Jesus showing his heart penetrated by a sword and surrounded by fire and a crown of thorns. Often the heart of Jesus was separated from the total person of Jesus Christ. We faithfully made the nine first Fridays and we bartered, as it were, with God that for such fidelity we would be surely guaranteed to die in grace and gain Heaven. Novenas to the Sacred Heart preceded our formal consecration to the Sacred Heart on the feast day in June. The official prayers of the church referred to the Sacred Heart as "It," always capitalized!

A CHANGING CULTURE

The devotion to the Sacred Heart, as it was practiced in our Catholic parishes and religious communities prior to Vatican II, was expressed in explicit symbols, and succeeded for the most part in meeting the religious needs of Catholics in nineteenth- and twentieth-century America and Europe because it integrated the affective life of the faithful and their basic culture into the faith life of the universal church. It was the predominantly accepted and, to some degree, most successful way of presenting to Catholics living in a "ghettoized" Catholicism the most fundamental truth of God's love for us— so great that he gave us his only begotten Son (Jn 3:16) as Love poured out on the cross that we might accept God's gift of salvation through Jesus crucified and be forgiven our sins. Without knowing too much about the technical, theological expressions of Christian salvation, devotees of the Sacred Heart of Jesus in those times found fashioned for metaphors of faith, symbols that responded both to their faith and to biblical traditions. Then, why and how did a devotion so pervasive in the church (including that in the United States) up until a quarter-century ago lose its popularity and effectiveness? We do not have the space here to trace the impact of revolutionary ideas upon the practice of this devotion and how it has changed.[17]

One key factor must be mentioned to explain this decline of devotion to the Sacred Heart as it had been practiced earlier: the "ghetto Catholicism" of the universal, Roman Catholic Church. In the United States, we Catholics were not yet fully integrated into the mainstream of American culture, which was still realizing itself as a unique entity. An inherited Roman Catholic piety, in parish life, devotions, practices, and the roles of nuns and priests as different from the silent laity, gave a definite cultural frame of reference, an assured identity, and security to such isolated individuals. But after World War II, Americans were melded into a nation with a common destiny, a challenge to overcome ghetto mentalities and to be "Americans" first and foremost.

Thus, as American Catholics entered into the mainstream of the nation's cultural life, they began to lose their enthusiasm for Catholic devotions that were so totally misunderstood by non-Catholics and even now by Catholics themselves. Small communities that gave us our identity as accepted and loved persons, such as the family, the small town, the civil community, and the parish, began to yield to a larger sense of belonging in which popular devotions offered little meaning to the individual identity. Advertising on radio, newspapers, and TV used religious symbols to sell products that would bring one worldly benefits, such as individual freedom, independent mobility, sexual prowess, and rising social status. Religious choral singing or classical music formed the background to picture a car and a nimbus or halo of soft, melting light like sunlight refracted through stained glass windows in an ancient cathedral, surrounded by a beautiful woman using Estée Lauder products.

The static symbols of God's love, especially a bleeding heart and a man who looks neither male nor female, but more like a strange creature, and not very human compared with the alluring images of attractive, bodied, true-to-life men and women on our TV screens, soon lost their appeal for Americanized Catholics. Intrinsic elements of this popular devotion lost their impact when they failed to meet American Catholics in a new, emerging culture that accentuated an evolutionary view of the world, as well as the need for deep, interpersonal relations to give one an identity.

Usually the faithful in their piety tended to look backwards in history instead of forward to an emergent world. They focused on Christ dying on the cross and pierced by the lance. The sad unmasculine face of Jesus in so many paintings and on statues of the Sacred Heart fostered much unhealthy sentimentality. Many of the specific practices were mechanical, such as that of the nine first Fridays, which presented an important element of Catholicism, and frequent reception of the Eucharist, which was popularly seen more as an insurance plan than the Source of transformation, a transformation that converts an ordinary individual into an apostle who will bring the Good News into the world.

A NEW UNDERSTANDING OF THE SYMBOL OF HEART

How can we in the Catholic Church, as we move into the third millennium of Christianity, recapture the essential elements of the traditional devotion to the Sacred Heart of Jesus, while leaving behind the elements that today are more obstacles than help to true devotion to Jesus, the Lover of mankind, even though they shaped the expression of devotional practices? The first step must be a greater understanding of the scriptural meaning of the symbol of heart and its relationship to the essential revealed truths of God's love for his children through the human-divine person of his only begotten Son, Jesus Christ, and his hidden Holy Spirit. Because of our "being-in-the-world," we are basically creatures who are not naturally focused upon God at all times in conscious awareness that he is our beginning and our end. We are being pulled in all directions by persons, things, and events that clamor for our attention. We need to have a "focus" in order that our deepest relationship with God may command the center of our consciousness and awareness, and thus exert maximum influence on our thoughts, words, and action.

Our human heart, as we have already seen in prior chapters, plays a role in Scripture, liturgy, and in common human relationship. The heart symbolizes our transcendence beyond the world, the inner stretching power within our spirit to go toward God and neighbor in thought and love. We are commanded to love God with our whole heart, our whole mind, our whole strength (Dt 6:6). Yahweh speaks through the prophet Jeremiah: "When you seek me you shall find me, when you seek me with all your heart: (Jer 29:13)

A DIVINE AND HUMAN HEART OF JESUS

We must move away from the limiting image of a merely biological human heart and advance toward a deeper expression of heart as the symbol of not only Jesus' human love for us unto a human death, but also of the perfect image of the Second Person of the Trinity, God from God, of one substance with the Father in his love for us as God, one with the Father and the Holy Spirit. The pierced heart of Jesus is the image of the total, self-emptying love of Jesus Christ, God-man, for each of us, made by God according to his image and likeness. But being one with the Father, Jesus' human heart is the image of the heavenly Father's love for us manifested through the Holy Spirit in the human heart of Christ. "To have seen me is to have seen the Father" (Jn 14:9). We are very scriptural when we use the heart of Jesus as the place, the focus where we encounter God, Trinity, in all their burning love for each of us. It is the place where we meet the triune God with all our strengths, God's gifts to us, but also with all our brokenness and sinfulness that cry out for healing form God. It is in the heart of Christ that the "new creation" or "the new person" is effected.

PRAYING AND EXPERIENCING THE TRINITY IN THE HEART OF JESUS

The second aspect of a new devotion to the Sacred Heart is that, through a larger understanding of the scriptural meaning of heart and the role of Jesus' humanity, symbolized as heart in loving self-giving to us human beings, we will no longer be focused on a self-centered, sentimental, privatized devotion to Jesus, our *ersatz* human lover. We will see our responsibility to die to our selfish ego in order to live crucified with Jesus to all that impedes our being loving members in his Body, the Church. Thus this second aspect would highlight Jesus as the Way, the Truth, and the Life (Jn 14:6) who reveals, in his personalized love for us, the personalized love of the Father and the hidden Holy Spirit. Knowledge, as experience of the "breadth and the length, the height and the depth" of the love of Christ that is beyond all knowledge (Eph 3:18), would come through the outpouring of his Spirit (Jn 7:37–39). That Spirit, when released in our hearts, would fulfill what Jesus promised: "The Advocate, the Holy Spirit, whom the Father will send in my name, will teach you everything and remind you of all I have said to you" (Jn 14:26). Above all, when we do not know how to pray in a deeper, surrendering way, the Spirit of Jesus comes to help us in our weakness. "the Spirit himself expresses our pleas in a way that could never be put into words" (Rm 8:27).

A third aspect of a new and truer devotion to the Sacred Heart of Jesus would consist in developing a passionate love for our material world and a sharing with Jesus, the risen Savior, to be his co-creators and ambassadors (2 Cor 5:18) in building our world into a loving community that will be coterminus with the total cosmic Christ in his bodied members. We strive with Christ to bring the world into its completion in his church through the mystical union of the Trinity with all of God's material creation.

Our culture today is rooted in nuclear physics that presents us with a material world in which even the subatomic particles are in intimate relationship with the fields of energy around them, and yet in which there is a superconsciousness directing matter from within toward a loving goal: the unity of all creatures in Jesus Christ and Jesus Christ in all things. For devotees of the Sacred Heart, the pulsating heart of Jesus Christ now becomes the personalized love that draws all things to himself. How beautifully Teilhard de Chardin in his classic *The Divine Milieu* describes the burning heart of Jesus as the center of all things:

> To have access to the divine milieu is to have found that one thing needful—Him who burns by setting fire to everything we would love badly or not enough; Him who calms by eclipsing with his blaze everything that we would love too much; Him

who consoles by gathering up everything that has been snatched from our love or has never been given to it. [18]

ABIDE IN ME AS I ABIDE IN YOU

We Christians, who have understood through the Spirit of love the infinite love of Jesus for each of us, will live more and more consciously in the intimate union with Christ as our guiding force. "Think of the love that the Father has lavished on us" (1 Jn 3:2). If Jesus, so full of love for you, truly abides within you, how can you ever again be lonely? How can you ever be focused solely on yourself and not completely on him, the burning center of love living within you and in the entire universe? Is it difficult for you now to keep in contact with him in his infinite, ever-now love for you unto death? No matter how weak you are, when you are aware of such a friend living within you, giving you courage to become one with him in all that you do and think and say, you can accomplish infinitely more that what you could do alone, "for cut off from me you can do nothing" (Jn 15:5). Peace and joy of the Spirit of Jesus govern all thought, words, and deeds—because you have experienced in him the infinite love of God. This love is not far away, but abides within your very heart, your deepest consciousness through the gifts of the Spirit of faith, hope, and love. No force outside can harm you "because you are from God and you have in you one who is greater than anyone in this world" (1 Jn 4:4).

TRUE DEVOTION TO JESUS CHRIST
AND THE SACRED HEART

True devotion to the Sacred Heart must be more than the experience of how much God loves you through the mirror of that love in Christ Jesus. One with Christ within you, you move out into your world around you. In loving obedient abandonment to Christ, you seek to live in love in every thought, word, and deed. You experience a continued growth in simplicity and freedom that approaches what Jesus himself experienced as he centered his whole earthly life on doing only the will of his Father.

Your personal whims and selfish feelings have no power now to determine your attitudes and ways of acting. Now you seek at all times to do only God's will in return for the infinite love he pours into your "heart" through the heart of Jesus. Your devotion to him in his loving heart is Measured by your love toward every man and woman you meet. You stretch out to share with Jesus Christ, the Lover of mankind, his great love for his world. His pierced heart becomes one with your heart, emptied out in loving service to fashion the world into the glorious total Christ.

PRAYER EXERCISE

1. Sit quietly in a darkened room. Light a candle and gaze at its soft, flickering light. Experience yourself becoming a part of that light. Realize this is a powerful symbol of Christ's interpenetration with your deepest layers of consciousness and even your unconscious. Feel the layers of inner darkness dissipate before the gentle touch of the light of love of the heavenly Father and the Holy Spirit, all dwelling within you.

2. Follow your deep breathing inward and gently let your breath go outward, Feel yourself relaxing on the physical, psychic, and spiritual levels of your being.

3. As you breathe deeply, hear Jesus, as the Center of your being, say gently, "Love Me."

4. Breathe out your breath gently as Jesus says, "As I love you."

5. Pause for a moment and realize that to love Jesus is to love your neighbor: "Whatsoever you did to the least of these brothers of mine, you did to me" (Mt 25:40).

6. Continue for twenty minutes, breathing in as Jesus says, "Love Me." Breathe out as Jesus says, "As I love you."

10

A Cosmic Heart

As modern citizens of the universe, with a nervous, often frantic, physical vitality—at times bordering on the brutal—we nevertheless betray our ancestral hunger for a life that no finite creature can finally satisfy. We stalk about our universe teeming with possibilities of greater life-experiences, with promises and prospects of fuller life and happiness. We are constantly reaching out for new thrills, yet we drop our hands empty at our sides. We gaze into seemingly infinite expanses of future possibilities. We are basically homeless, as we wander through a void that yields nothing of its dark secrets to us.

In our modern age, scientific discoveries have opened to us a world of almost infinite complexity. As we face an ever-expanding universe, we fear that which we cannot dominate. We feel that we are swimming desperately in an ocean of opposing forces that we cannot dominate. We feel our own inability to make out of the amorphous mass of created beings around us an integral part of our own reality.

For those of us who believe in a God who transcends this sense world, or for the confused and frustrated of us who would like to believe in something or someone bigger or more enduring than this fleeting pleasure or that past joy, there is a desire or an unexpressed hope to approach such a transcendent Being immediately. Rituals and rites, symbols and priests, have apparently lost most of their usefulness for the young generation.

The modern Christian experiences a greater conflict, perhaps, than the non-Christian in her/his conscience. The nihilistic void of modern existence contradicts the basic beliefs of one's Christian faith. We are not necessarily aided by our creed in solving everyday problems. In our customary devotional practices, God seems so far away and the world so close! So many of us are caught in a religious view that had been given to us in our younger years that presents itself to us as a flight into another world. It is difficult to reconcile such a view with our strong attraction to the world that fills us with a tense love-hate attitude to the world and to God, which we believe to be in complete contradiction to each other.

IS JESUS CHRIST STILL RELEVANT?

Our age presents modern Christians with a religious crisis that ultimately centers on the person of Jesus Christ. Does the Christ traditionally presented to us in religion classes and Sunday sermons have relevance for us, absorbed as we are in fashioning a new and exciting world? How can we find him, the Source of all life, in this complex, ever-changing world? Can we touch the heart of Christ in our cosmos today?

Surely as Christians we must reject any view of Christianity as based on an "other-worldly" spirituality. Diettrich Bonhoeffer, the German Lutheran minister put to death by the Nazis at the age of thirty-nine in 1945, captured the modern attitude toward a religion of flight:

> Other-worldliness affords a splendid environment in which to live. Whenever life begins to become oppressive and troublesome, a person just leaps into the air with a bold kick and soars relieved and unencumbered into so-called eternal fields. He leaps over the present. He disdains the earth; he is better than it. After

all, besides the temporal defeats he still has eternal victories, and they are so easily achieved. Other-worldliness also makes it easy to preach and to speak words of comfort. An other-worldly Church can be certain that it will in no time win over all the weaklings, all who are only too glad to be deceived and deluded, all utopianists. . . . Man is weak, that's just the way he is; and this weakling man is open to the religion of other-worldliness. Should it be denied him? Should the weakling remain without help? . . . No, the weak man should receive help. He does not lead man in a religious flight from this world to other worlds beyond; rather, he gives him back to the earth as its loyal son.[1]

SECULARISM

The opposite reaction that we see all about us in our modern culture, equally arising from a distrust that God's kingdom could be really relevant to this world, is a complete immersion in this world as the total *milieu* of our human existence. Such a belief includes an extreme optimism that trusts solely in human resourcefulness to create by our human efforts a "lasting city" on this earth. The promise of such utopian "secularism" is that all religions, including Christianity, are irrelevant for the only "world" there is.

Recent Christian thought reveals a reaction both to other-worldly spirituality and to utopian secularism. Led by Maurice Blondel, such writers as Henri de Lubac, Hans Ur von Balthasar, and Karl Rahner stress the unity between God and his world, between the supernatural and the natural, between grace and nature. Starting with an optimistic vision of God's dominion over his created world and a trust that he could and would attain the end that he intended in creating this world, these thinkers have insisted that God was to be encountered precisely in and through the world–the world God has always looked at and seen as "very good" (Gn 1:31).

God so loved this world as to give his only begotten Son who came to establish his kingdom on this earth. This kingdom, wherein Christ becomes present to his creatures, is hidden within the material world, like leaven in a mass of dough. Father shows us Christ immanently working to transform and complete God's creation. Instead of fleeing the material world, we are to encounter Christ there. All created beings exist through Christ and are sustained in their being by Christ's activity.

He is the *Logos*, the image according to which not only man and woman are made, but all creation is fashioned. Through him all creatures will attain their completion. "All things came into being through him, and without him there came to be not one thing that has come to be" (Jn 1:3). "In him were created all creatures in the heavens and on the earth. . . . all have been created through him and for him" (Col 1:16–17).

St. Paul more than any other early sacred writer beheld Christ immersed in and energizing the created, material world. In his captivity letters, Christ is shown as the center of unity for all that has been created. Paul would wish to lead us high up on the mountain of faith to gaze over the whole universe below. If we share his faith, we shall see Christ as the center and focal point toward whom and from whom all beings flow, verifying Heidegger's insight that truth is ultimately full reality. All beings have their ontological intelligibility and are "true" to the degree that their relationship "in being" to Ultimate Reality is comprehended.

Christ is not, therefore, to be separated from material reality. All reality is already christologically structured by the incarnation whereby God has inserted himself into his creation.

CHRISTIAN SECULARITY

To avoid a mistaken "incarnational" optimism that would depict Christ as undergoing a series of "incarnations" in our world completely independent of the activities of human beings, a more recent current of thought has evolved. This school of thought is best described as Christian secularity. It is not to be confused with secularism; rather, it is just the opposite, and stands as the main modern answer to it. Some of the leading Catholic proponents of this new thought are Karl Rahner, Teilhard de Chardin, Johannes Metz, Gustave Thils, J. Mouroux, Walter Ong, Yves Congar, M.-D. Chenu, and E. Schillebeecks.

Christian secularity begins with this real, "secular," not-godly world. Into this world God sent his own Son to communicate with mankind through his material world. Matter is sacred insofar as it is precisely in Christ's humanity, which is not the infinite, sacred God, the fullness of being, but is worldly, distinct from God, finite, dependent on God for its existence, that God can reveal his great goodness and love. Through Christ, God communicates his being to something other than himself.

In the Incarnation, humanity reaches its fullness and perfection, because through Christ's humanity "worldly," non-godly humanity is united, through God's infinite act of love, with God himself; in the hypostatic union, human nature receives the existence of God in the person of Jesus Christ. His humanity remains humanity. It is never swallowed up or sacralized. Yet the humanity of Christ, especially in his human consciousness, reaches the maximum of self-transcendence. The human nature of Christ in the intimate divine communication within itself reaches its fullness of being. All its capacities, potentialities, as created by God, are complete in sharing God's life.

GOD'S PERFECT SELF-GIVING TO US IN CHRIST

But the historical Christ is more than the apogee of humanity. This truth, if pressed too far, could circle back to the Arian heresy, which so exalted the humanity of Christ that it denied his divinity. Christ is, as Karl Rahner expresses, it, even more than the peak of cosmic realities. He becomes the goal toward which the whole cosmos is moving and in whom the cosmos will find its completion. In Christ we have God's gift of himself to us, irreversible given. God can never withdraw his self-giving because he is not incarnated in the living person, Jesus Christ.

God has given himself to us through other finite creatures by giving extrinsically of his perfections in a finite, imperfect, participated mode of existence. But now God has a human heart! It is the heart of the God-man, Jesus Christ, who loves both the Father and us with the same heart.

The mystery of the Incarnation reveals God's intrinsic giving of himself, the gift of his very inner Life, his divine-human heart, to us human beings in a visible, human for, an autonomous, human consciousness, that can never be reversed or extinguished.

Briefly stated, therefore, through the hypostatic union, in an historical event that unfolded in space and time in the Incarnation of the second person of the Trinity, God has given himself totally to us. If God has given himself irreversible to us through Christ, then Christ must be, not only God's instrument, but God himself. The promise of God to give himself to us absolutely is realized completely and irreversibly in the hypostatic union. E. Schillebeecks succinctly summarizes the union of divinity and humanity, of matter and spirit, of heaven and earth, brought about by the hypostatic union:

> In Christ, and through him, human existence has become the objective expression of God's absolute communication of himself to man, and by the same token, the objective expression of the human response to that total divine gift. . . . The human existence of Christ, taken with all its determinism and all its human implications, is the personal life of God, the Son. This means that the entire temporal dimension and the unabridged reality we call profane can be assumed into a God-related life,

given that in the Son the eternal has presented itself personally within temporal and terrestrial realities. The very definition of the hypostatic union is exactly that. This also reveals the fact that, thanks to Christ all of human history is swathed in God's love; it is assumed into the absolute and gratuitous presence of the mystery of God. The worldly and the temporal remain worldly and temporal; they are not sacralized but sanctified by that presence, that is, by the God-centered life of Christ and of his faithful.[2]

CALL TO RESPOND TO GOD'S OUTPOURED LOVE IN CHRIST

Thus, we see that we human beings and the whole concrete world are dependent on Christ for our fullness of actuated being. The world has been given to us as a manifestation of the love that God has for each of us. This does not mean that we are to regard the material things of this world only as "instruments " for the spread of the kingdom of God. We have seen already that each material creature has its own intrinsic value and proper relationship to Christ, its own finality. But its full completion cannot be attained unless we, made to God's image and likeness, inasmuch as we possess an intellect to know God's love and a will to respond, unite our heart with the heart of Christ through our creative powers to fashion this universe into a conscious reflection of God's inner beauty. As co-creator with the immanent divine Logos-made-flesh, Jesus Christ, present within the cosmos, through the "game" of the resurrection, as Teilhard de Chardin expressed the immanence of the risen Christ, we are to achieve the fullness of our true being in him. Christ is still loving and cooperating with us in the restoration of communion, first over ourselves and then over the non-human cosmos, a truth often forgotten by many theologians and spiritual writers today. But this was the most evident and viable truth grasped by the early Christians, and it led to the Chalcedonian definition that provided the basic teaching for an integral Christology.[3]

To believe that we can find God only in retreat from modern society is to disbelieve that God is all-loving and all-powerful. He does want to reveal himself to us through his living Word-made-flesh, Jesus Christ, as we find Christ inserted actively inside every part of our present world. Amos Wilder insists that we discover God as *Grace* within the context of our present world:

> If we are to have any transcendence today, even Christian, it must be in and through the secular. . . . If we are to find *Grace* it is to be found in the world and not overhead. The sublime firmament of overhead reality that provided a spiritual home for the souls of men until the eighteenth century has collapsed.[4]

DISCOVERING THE COSMIC CHRIST

But how does a Christian find Jesus Christ shining "diaphanously," as Teilhard de Chardin expressed it, through our material world today? The architects of a theology of the cosmic Christ that contemplated the risen Lord inside of the material world, exerting his power of reconciling all things back to the Father by bringing the whole created order into its fullness through his living members of his Body, the Church, can be found in the writings of Paul and John of the New Testament and of the early Eastern Fathers of the Church as Irenaeus, Clement, Origen, Athanasius, Basil, Gregory of Nazianzus and Gregory of Nyssa, Cyril of Alexandria, and Maximus the Confessor.[5]

Such an early vision of Christ's cosmic presence faded away through the Middle Ages, especially in the writings of the Western Scholastic theologians. Pierre Teilhard de Chardin, through his scientific research as a leading paleontologist of the twentieth century, his philosophical and theological studies as a Jesuit priest, and above all, through his own striking integration of these diverse roles in an extraordinary, mystical personality, has succeeded in expressing it in terms that we modern citizens of the universe can better understand and make a part of our living experience.

LOVE OF GOD AND NEIGHBOR

To discover the cosmic heart of Christ and to surrender to his loving, creative Spirit dwelling within us as we live and work in and with Christ to fashion the universe into the total Christ, "and through him to reconcile all things for him" (Col 1:20), let us begin with the insight of Karl Rahner on the unity between the love of God and neighbor. In the preceding chapters, we have dwelt upon the deeper meaning of heart as the unity-in-difference of all our created humanity on body, soul, and spirit levels where we are freest to surrender our life in all our choices according to the mind or heart of Christ. We then developed how we can live at the center of our true self in Christ by praying always in our heart. In Chapter 9 we sought to highlight the meaning of devotion to the heart of Christ.

We must not succumb to the temptation of centering into an affective union between ourselves and the indwelling Christ on an exclusive vertical relationship whereby we disregard the horizontal, social dimension of loving in action also our neighbors. Let us see this social dimension of ourselves in union with the heart of Christ turned toward other human beings and in the entire created world. We can agree with commentators of Karl Rahner's theology, such as Dr. Annice Callahan,[6] that the social dimension has been somewhat neglected by Rahner, at least as a practical call to struggle to liberate the oppressed and the poor of the world.

However, Rahner does develop the social dimension almost exclusively on the ecclesial dimension through his treatment of the theme of the unity of the love of God and neighbor.

Rahner gives us a principle to validate the unity between the love of God and neighbor. To speak of the human person is to speak of God and vice versa.[7] To speak of the human person is already to learn something about God, since all of us are oriented by our nature to the absolute mystery, who is God.[8]

By the incarnation, God's transcendence and absolute mystery has become immanent and his unconditional love can now be experienced through the heart of Christ, who brings a unity-in-difference to his perfect love of the Father and his image of God's perfect love for his children in his complete self-sacrificing love for his neighbor, which means all of us.

In our daily living out of the two great commandments, what has separated our love for God from our love for our neighbor has been our failure to accept the unity in love of God and neighbor to which the heart of Christ opens us to receive and be transformed. As he loves us at the core of our deepest consciousness, infused by the Spirit's faith, hope, and love, he effects by his Spirit the divinization or transformation of ourselves into loving children of God, brothers and sisters to our Brother and Neighbor, Jesus Christ.

BE LOVE

As Jesus has loved his neighbors, who came into his earthly life, including his enemies, through the unity-in-difference of his burning love for his Father, so we, too, can love God in and with Jesus Christ with our "whole heart, soul, mind and strength" (Dt 6:7; Mt 22:34–40). But we can also, as a result of our transformation by the Spirit's love, love our neighbor as we love ourselves. Love of neighbor must not be regarded as a virtue among other virtues that we are obligated to perform in order to attain a heavenly reward. It is rather the state of being transformed by the love of God that abounds in our hearts through the Spirit (Rm 5:5). Rahner sees love of neighbor as the principle of the act of love of God. This Jesus proved in his human relations to God and neighbor in the Gospels. Rahner writes: "One can love God whom one does not see only by loving one's visible brother lovingly."[9]

INVOLVING LOVE

As you touch God more intimately, see him as immediately present and indwelling within your very being, you are more intimately drawn to a union of love toward your neighbor through active, loving service. St. Dorotheus of the sixth century used the example of a wheel. The closer the spokes of the wheel move toward the center, the closer they come to each other. The farther they move out from center, the more distance separates one spoke from another.

Today more than ever with the communication media allowing us to be "present" to billions of people around the world, no Christian can avoid concern with the rampant poverty—physical, psychic, and spiritual—that covers most human beings like a suffocating black cloud. We cannot muffle our ears and block out the cries of our suffering brothers and sisters, wherever in the world there may be victims of oppression, wars, or natural calamities.

Dr. Albert Schweitzer said repeatedly that so long as there was a single person in the world who was hungry, sick, lonely, or living in fear, that person was his responsibility. This is to live out what Jesus taught his disciples: "I tell you solemnly, insofar as you did this to one of the least of these brothers of mine, you did it to me" (Mt 25:40).

As Christians, we know that our faith in God's love for us and our "affective" return of that love to God by words alone are dead without an effective involvement in manifesting unselfish love to others in need. This was the constant persuasion among the early Christians as James wrote in his epistle:

If one of the brothers or one of the sisters is in need of clothes and has not enough food to live on, and one of you says to him, "I wish you well, keep yourself warm and eat plenty," without giving him these bare necessities of life, then what good is that? Faith is like that; if good works do not go with it, it is quite dead. (Jas 2:15–17)

A LOVING CONCERN FOR OTHERS

Through our deep, involving love shown toward one other person, be it God or neighbor, we come to learn that true, agapic love cannot be turned inward in an exclusive way. It breaks out toward a larger community where we find our love growing as we assume responsibility for the happiness of our brothers and sisters. If our prayer is authentic and deeply transforming, if we are truly living in the presence of God's intimate, unselfish love for us, we will be turned toward others, especially those who have the greatest need—physical, psychic, and spiritual.

The Christian principle is always: "No one has ever seen God. Yet if we love one another, God remains in us, and his love is brought to perfection in us" (1 Jn 4:12). Yet how we will release God's love, as an intimately concerned God for his children, will depend greatly on our individual talents and state of life. But openness to the world community is the sign of love as a growing process of our leading others to find their true identity as beautiful, worthwhile persons.

Gabriel Marcel characterizes what our true love should be like toward God and neighbor. It is basically characterized by *availability, mutuality,* and the readiness to *sacrifice* oneself by readiness to suffer the cross in passing over from selfishness to unconditional love for others.[10]

These are the characteristics of the heart of Jesus in loving us. But we need a theological perspective that is expressed in terms of an evolving process, since we live now in an age of nuclear physics. In such a dynamic view of all created things as fields of energies, we see each individual component in a relational movement toward greater complexity and consciousness in a loving unity-in-difference.

PIERRE TEILHARD DE CHARDIN

No modern writer brings together, with a personal passionate love for Christ and also the material cosmos, a cosmic synthesis so well as Teilhard de Chardin has done. He realized within himself and within the hearts of all modern human beings a tension between the love of Christ and one's love for a world in evolution. In a letter of 1916, Teilhard confesses his burning desire to reconcile these two tensioned loves:

> I want to love Christ . . . in the very act of loving the universe.
> . . . Besides communion with God and communion with the world, is there not also communion with God in and through the earth? I should like it to be so, for myself and for many others.[11]

Teilhard wanted to bring about a unification-in-difference of these two attracting poles of loves in a way that the Christian could be dedicated to the world and in that very dedication consecrate him/herself to Christ.

His greatest contribution was to outline the universe as permeated by the delicate hand of the Holy Spirit giving order to the universe. This Spirit permeates all of creation through our human cooperation with the immanent, personalized risen Jesus Christ and effectively spiritualizes the cosmos by bringing all of creation to the personalized, central point that Teilhard calls the "Omega Point."

OMEGA POINT

What is this point of union, this point of convergence toward which all matter, all human beings are moving? The process of moving through space and time is likened by Teilhard to a cone. The tip or point of the cone Teilhard calls "Omega." This is the goal toward which evolution is moving, the point of convergence of all inferior lines that meet in it.

Before Teilhard identifies this Omega Point with the risen and cosmic Christ, he describes the three characteristics of Omega Point. (1) It must be of an objective nature. As real as the process of evolution and the laws of its development, so too must be the end or goal toward which it is moving. (2) It must have the power in itself to draw or attract by its own activity all creatures into a unity to their full consummation. To draw intellectual beings, this point of attraction must also be an intellectual being, a person. He must draw as a person through his goodness, beauty, and perfect love until self-sacrifice. (3) It must be able to move the whole universe to its united perfection without any fear of regression, destruction, or total frustration.[12]

Teilhard insists that his cosmic Christ is the Christ of the Gospels. This Center operates on both levels with distinction, but not separation, in a unity-in-difference, between the natural and supernatural. As human beings we can reach our fulfillment in the cosmic Christ by our cooperation in living under his guiding Spirit. Yet the supernatural fullness of Christ in the *pleroma* or full manifestation of God's created world in and for Christ is being formed by the re-creation of the natural.

He stresses in his writings that through the incarnation, death, and resurrection, the Word made flesh has inserted himself within our material "natural" universe and has become the cosmic Center drawing all beings, now elevated by the gratuitous loving activity of the Trinity, to a united destiny around the supernatural Center, Christ, the "Omega Point."[13]

THE COSMIC OR CHRISTIC NATURE

What does Teilhard mean when he says that Christ is literally the "physical" Center of this expanding universe? We often understand the word "physical" as synonymous with "material." *Physical* as used by Teilhard has some of the nuance and breadth of the term as used by the early Greek Fathers. *Phusis* means nature, but not in a strictly metaphysical sense. Perhaps "reality" or "ontological reality" would be a better way to translate Teilhard's sense of physical. It would thus signify, not only a given being in its present existence and metaphysical constituent parts, but, above all, it includes total being in its dynamic progression toward fulfillment.

Its perfect fulfillment coincides with God's finality which is the purpose for God's immanent activity in creatures. What makes up an essential part contributing to the full "reality" of a given human being is the continuity that joins the Head and the members, Christ and us, and effects the individual divinization that is our fullness, flowing out into the collective divinization.

Thus, not only body and soul, matter and spirit, make up the physical human person, but the real, ontological being would find its physical fullness only in a *divinization* of his whole being by the indwelling of the Trinity. Union with Christ through grace leading to an immanent union with the Trinity, for Teilhard as well as for the early Eastern Fathers, was a "physical" union, meaning both ontologically real and according to the fullness of our created potencies. Our God-given nature (*phusis*) has always been destined by God to be a christified nature through sanctifying grace. Thus the real human being would be the full person with all human potentialities fulfilled only in and through Christ who alone could actuate our true being to become, finally, filiated to the Father as a divinized daughter or son of God, not by our own nature, but, as Peter writes, as a "participator in the divine nature" (2 Pt 1:4).

A PHYLUM OF SALVATION

Through this body of christified persons, Christ reaches the rest of humankind and the material universe. Teilhard develops his concept of the growing Body-Person Christ in terms of his cosmic vision. The christified, the new Israel's People of God, is a "phylum of salvation" that spreads its inner life and hyper-personalism (engendered by the life of the physical Body-Person of Christ) in a movement of greater consciousness, always ascending until the completion of the total body in the parousia, the second coming in Christ's full manifestation of unity-in-difference. In his book *Phenomenon of Man*, Teilhard compares the Christian "leaven" to a phylum that, through greater consciousness, moves toward as unity effected by love of many in oneness without destroying the uniqueness of each person in this unified body of Christ. This consciousness reaches our fullness in the spiritual relationship of love to the transcendent pole of the whole universal process of convergence, and that is Jesus Christ.[14]

Christ is the evolver of this super-humanity. He makes his members' love or charity "universalized," "energized," and synthesized.[15]

This charity is universalized because christified individuals find God lovable in all creatures and events. The diaphany of God shines through the material universe. The world becomes charged with God's loving presence. Through the interpenetration of the divine presence throughout the material world, the cosmos no longer is an obstacle to the vision of God, but rather it becomes the mirror in which we see God. It becomes the "milieu" in which we can enjoy a constant and universal communion with the cosmic heart of Christ.[16]

A COSMIC HUMAN HEART

Our charity toward our neighbors becomes energized by our oneness with the cosmic heart of Christ into an active love proved by deeds. No longer content with a glance of commiseration or a vague desire to reduce the evil in the world, we are now activated to bring the whole of humanity to a greater consciousness. We approach Christ and grasp him in our efforts to perfect and unify all in him. To help form Christ in others is the greatest act of charity that we can do.

Finally, our charity becomes unified or synthesized. A great part of our life lacks true charity as its impelling motive for action. So often our contact with material creatures or with our fellow human beings is motivated by self-interest or utility. But when, through conscious reflection, we center ourselves and all our activities on the central reality of Christ, the Evolver of the universe toward whom and in whom the whole universe is converging, then the mass of our activities becomes synthesized.

Teilhard insists that only when we give to all of our disparate actions a "psychic" character, a person-to-person, center-to-center, an intimate heart-to-heart relationship between ourselves and the depths of the cosmic Christ as risen and inserted into the universe, will our lives be meaningful. Our innermost energies are transformed and sublimated within "the field of the Omega."[17]

Christ alone is the center and the goal of our universe. The more we become conscious of Christ's presence at the very heart of the earth, as we have become also conscious primarily of his presence in the depths of our heart, at the core of our being, in affective surrender to him as Lord, the more beautiful creation becomes. This is the preparation with our cooperative creativity permeated by Grace, God's uncreated energies of divine love, Father, Son, and Holy Spirit, of the mystical body worthy of resurrection into a full participation of the life that is already his at the center of our created world.

HASTENING THE PAROUSIA OF CHRIST

The process of the evolving universe goes forward and upward at the same time. And inserted within this total process, guided always by Christ to the fullness that will presage his *parousia*, is the phylum of salvation, the church, those members of Christ who, through detachment, exenteration, embracing the cross by loving self-sacrifice toward others, have rendered themselves "passionately indifferent" to everything but Christ. Then St. Paul's prophetic statement will be fulfilled: "There is only Christ: he is everything and he is in everything" (Col 3:11).

Christ is being formed in us. His cosmic heart is becoming one with our human heart in a very real, ontological way as we yield ourselves more perfectly to his direction. Charged with the living presence of Christ within us, we christified human beings, living within an expanding universe, extend the process of christification to hasten the day when the lines of the evolving universe and the evolving Christ in his members will converge in the Omega Point. Then we will understand Paul's summation of the universe and God's eternal plan in Christ Jesus: "For it pleased God the Father that in him all fullness should dwell, and that through him God should reconcile to himself every being, and make peace both on earth and in heaven through the blood shed on the cross" (Col 1:19–20).

Then Teilhard's prayer to Christ will have become realized as our heart is one with the heart of Christ:

> And then, my Lord, enfold me in the depths of thy heart. And there keep me, refine, purge, kindle, set on fire, raise aloft, according to the most pure desire of thy heart, and for my cleansing extinction.[18]

CONCLUSION

Science can offer to us a world of great potentiality, surging ever forward in a dynamic movement to greater complexity in unity. It can present to us an objective world of reflected beauty and quasi-order that allows us by faith to come to know much that is objective about the infinite and inexhaustible power and perfect love we call God.

Yet the aim we have proposed to offer in this book is to develop, as a complement to science and a speculative theology of clear and distinct ideas about God, another true and more sublime knowledge: that of the *heart*. Such a knowledge is given to the "pure of heart," who, purified from the illusions of their independence of God and separation from other creatures, open up to God's self-emptying (*kenotic*) love, the Holy Spirit. It is the Spirit who reveals immediately to the "poor in spirit" the very heart of God by knowing the mind and heart of the Word-made-flesh, Jesus Christ.

To those human beings who walk with humility of heart and integration before God-Trinity (Mi 6:8), the heart of Christ is discovered as an open, pierced heart of Jesus on the cross. It is through this emptied heart on the cross that the small bank of "little people," God's *Anawim*, can find an entrance into the depths of God's very being as emptied love for each of us, his children.

In that pierced heart we can also discover the perfect love of God for all of his creation in and through his Logos-made-flesh and his Spirit. We can touch the cosmic heart of Christ, but only as we live in the depths of our true being, our heart, in a unity-in-difference with the heart of Christ. Deep calls to deep. Heart calls to heart. How deeply your heart has entered into the heart of Christ, how much of God's fire of love you have allowed to touch yourself is measured by how much fiery love you show in service to others.

We are called by God-Trinity to be cooperators to explicitly draw out the core of inner fire, of God's love at the heart of all matter. The more we can act with full consciousness and reflection, the more we humanize ourselves, and the more we unleash the spiritual powers that enable us to transcend the material, the limited, the particular, and pass over to the realm of enduring and limitless spirit.

We are privileged by God's call to manifest his heart of healing love to the broken and downhearted. This can come about by living in our heart within the heart of Christ as we bring his flaming heart into this cosmos by unveiling the cosmic heart of Christ in our oneness with him to make it possible that he might enfold, like a nurturing mother, the universe God has created as a mirror reflecting a perfect, humble, all-powerful love. This love is experienced as a pierced heart, poured out, that we human beings may also be a heart pierced by divine love to be love for each other and all of God's cosmos as we assist in the birthing of the universe into the total, cosmic Christ, and help to reconcile the universe to the Father through his Son in his Spirit.

Notes

Chapter One

1. "Who Is God?" *Life Magazine* (December 1990), p. 54.

2. Maria F. Mahoney, *The Meaning in Dreams and Dreaming* (Secaucus, NJ: The Citadel Press, 1976), p. 138.

3. Carlos Castaneda, *Journey to Ixtlan* (New York: Simon & Schuster, 1972), p. 299.

4. Rudolf Otto, *The Idea of the Holy*, tr. J. W. Harvey (New York: Oxford University Press, 1958), pp. 5–11.

5. Dietrich Von Hildebrand, *The Sacred Heart: Source of Christian Affectivity* (Baltimore: Helicon, 1965), p. 26.

6. *"Le coeur a ses raison que la raison ne connait pas."*

7. St. Thomas Aquinas, *Summa Theologiae, Prima Pars,* 13, 7 ad 4.

8. E. S. Gausted, *Dissent in American Religion* (Chicago: University of Chicago Press, 1973), p. 149.

9. *Ibid.*, pp. 150–51.

Chapter Two

1. Dag Hammarskjold, *Markings,* tr. Leif Sjoberg and W. H. Auden (London: Faber & Faber, 1964), p. 56.

2. T. S. Eliot, "The Hollow Men," *The Complete Poems and Plays 1909–1950* (New York: Harcourt Brace and World, 1962), pp. 58–59.

3. V. E. Frankl, *La psychotherapie et son image de l' homme* (Paris, 1970), p. 150.

4. Sam Keen, *Apology for Wonder* (New York: Harper & Row, 1969).

5. *Ibid.*, pp. 13–49.

Chapter Three

1. Thomas Kuhn, *The Structure of Scientific Revolutions*, 2nd ed. (Chicago: University of Chicago Press, 1970).

2. Dr. Willis Harman has developed another approach in *Global Mind Change* (Indianapolis: Knowledge Systems, Inc., 1988). See George A. Maloney, S.J., *Mysticism and the New Age: Christic Consciousness in the New Creation* (Staten Island: Alba House, 1991), pp. 11–14.

3. Lewis Mumford, *The Transfiguration of Man* (New York: Harper Bros., 1956), p. 231.

4. Jean Gebser, *The Ever-Present Origin,* cited by Hugo Enomiya-Lassalle, *Living in the New Consciousness* (Boston: Shambala, 1988), p. 54.

5. Hugo Enomiya-Lassalle, S.J., who spent most of his Jesuit life in Japan seeking to harmonize Christianity and Zen Buddhism on the levels of mystical consciousness, especially in his work, *Living in the New Consciousness,* trans. from the German by Paul Shepherd (Boston; Shambala, 1988).

6. Dr. Karl Jaspers, *The Origin and Goal of History* (New Haven: Yale University Press, 1953). See also William M. Thompson, *Christ and Consciousness* (New York: Paulist Press, 1977), pp. 20–23.

7. Albert Einstein, *The World As I See It,* tr. Alan Harris (New York: Harper Bros., 1949), p. 5.

8. Lassalle, *op. cit.,* p. 32.

9. Teilhard de Chardin, *The Divine Milieu,* tr. B. Wall (New York: Harper Bros., 1960), p. 110.

10. St. Maximus, *The Four Centuries on Charity,* Bk. I, 95, tr. Polycarp Sherwood, O.S.B., in *Ancient Christian Writers,* Vol. XXI (Westminster, MD: Newman, 1955), p. 151.

Chapter Four

1. *Yes, Virginia, There Really Is a Santa Claus* (New York: Elizabeth Press, 1972), p. 7.

2. *Upanishads du Yoga,* tr. and ed. Jean Varenne (Paris, 1971), cited in Michel Meslin, "Heart," *The Encyclopedia of Religion* (New York: Macmillan & Free Press, 1987), p. 234.

3. G. A. Maloney, *Man—The Divine Icon* (Pecos, NM: Dove Press, 1974), pp. 55ff.

4. Irenaeus, *Adversus Haereses* V, 9: 1–3 in *The Ante-Nicene Fathers,* Vol. 1, eds. A. Roberts and J. Donaldson (Grand Rapids, MI: Eerdman, n.d.), pp. 531–32.

5. Most modern commentators on this text point out that the Greek word used for "life" is *psyche,* but is equivalent to the Hebrew *nephesh* and means all three senses of *life, soul,* and *person.*

6. For a complete view of Eastern Christian *hesychasm,* see George A. Maloney, S.J., *Russian Hesychasm* (The Hague: Mouton, 1973).

7. For a review of the latest scholarship on this anonymous writer who had so much influence on Christian piety and for a new translation of his *Spiritual Homilies,* see George A. Maloney, S.J., *Intoxicated with God. The 50 Spiritual Homilies of Macarius* (Denville, NJ: Dimension Books, 1978).

8. Macarius, *Spiritual Homilies, op. cit.,* p. 100.

9. St. Theophan the Recluse, cited in *The Art of Prayer*, compiled by Igumen Chariton, tr. E. Kadloubovsky and G. E. H. Palmer (London: Faber & Faber, 1966), pp. 190–91.

10. Macarius, *Spiritual Homilies, op. cit.,* Homily 15, p. 104.

11. For further development on the practice of breathing, see *Silence of Breath,* ed. R. Ballentine, M.D. (Glenview, IL: The Himalayan Institute, 1976); Brahmachari Amaldas, *Yoga and Contemplation* (Trichy, Tamilnadu, India: Shantivanam Ashram, 1974); Sister Vandana, *Nama Japa, The Prayer of the Name* (Bombay: Bharatiya Vidya Bhavan, 1984); Karlfried Graf von Durckheim, *Hara: The Vital Centre of Man* (London: George Allen & Unwin, Ltd., 1973).

Chapter Five

1. Bernard Lonergan, S.J., "Theology in Its New Context," in *Theology of Renewal,* Vol. I, ed. L. K. Shook (Montreal: Palm Publishers, 1968), pp. 44–45.

2. Thomas Merton, *A Thomas Merton Reader,* ed. Thomas B. McConnell (New York: Harcourt Brace and World, 1962), quoted by Paul

V. Robb, S.J., "Conversion as a Human Experience," in *Studies in the Spirituality of Jesuits* (St. Louis, MO, 1982), Vol. XIV, no. 3, p. 4.

3. Karl Rahner, *Everyday Faith* (New York: Sheed & Ward, 1968), p. 112.

4. Nikos Kazantzakis, *Report to El Greco* (New York: Simon and Schuster, 1958), p. 23.

5. Dag Hammarskjold, *Markings,* tr. Leif Sjoberg and W. H. Auden (London: Faber & Faber, 1964), p. 58.

6. Gregory of Nyssa, *On Virginity, PG* 46, 352 A–D, cited in *From Glory to Glory,* eds. J. Danielou and H. Musurillo (New York: Scribner, 1961), pp. 102–103.

7. Thomas Merton, *The Climate of Monastic Prayer* (Spencer, MA: Cistercian Press, 1969), p. 128.

Chapter Six

1. Carlos Castaneda, *Journey to Ixtlan* (New York: Simon & Schuster, 1972), p. 199.

2. Paul Tillich, *The Courage To Be* (New Haven: Yale University Press, 1952), pp. 39–66.

3. Carlos Castaneda, *A Separate Reality* (New York: Simon & Schuster, 1971), p. 43.

4. Gabriel Marcel, *Problematic Man,* tr. Brian Thompson (New York: Herder & Herder, 1967), p. 53.

5. *Ibid.,* p. 100.

6. Rainer Maria Rilke, *Letter 74: Briefe aus den Jahren 1907 bis 1914,* cited by Rollo May, *Love and Will* (New York: Dell Publishing Co., Inc., 1969), p. 122.

7. Rollo May, *op. cit.,* p. 139.

8. Dr. William Kraft, *A Psychology of Nothingness* (Philadelphia: Westminster Press, 1974), p. 28.

9. Dr. Carl Rogers, *On Becoming a Person* (Boston: Houghton Mifflin Co., 1961), p. 171.

10. This poem was first published in a collection of my poetic meditations entitled *The Returning Sun: Hope for a Broken World* (Locust Valley, NY: Living Flame, 1982), p. 42.

Chapter Seven

1. William of St. Thierry, *On the Solitary Life*, cited by M. Dechanet, *Yoga and God* (St. Meinrad, IN: Abbey Press, 1975), pp. 10–11.
2. Bernard Lonergan, S.J., *Method in Theology*, 2nd ed. (New York: Herder & Herder, 1972), p. 109.
3. St. Gregory of Nyssa, *Beatitudes*, PG 44; 1228, Sermon 3.
4. Cf. Lawrence LeShan, *You Can Fight for Your Life: Emotional Factors in the Causation of Cancer* (New York: M. Evans, Inc., 1977).
5. Ira Progoff: *The Symbolic and the Real* (New York: McGraw-Hill Book Co., 1963), pp. 69–75.
6. For a detailed presentation of Christian trust in God's active, providential love in our lives, see George A. Maloney, S.J., *In Jesus We Trust* (Notre Dame, IN: Ave Maria Press, 1990).
7. Carl Jung, *Modern Man in Search of a Soul* (London: K. Paul, Trench & Trubner, 1933), p. 259.
8. Dr. Karlfried Graf Dürckheim: *The Way of Transformation* (London: Unwin Paperbacks, 1980), pp. 37–38.

Chapter Eight

1. *The Art of Prayer*, complied by Igumen Chariton of Valamo, tr. E. Kadloubovsky and E. M. Palmer (London: Faber & Faber, 1966), p. 47.
2. John Cassian, *Conferences*, 10, ch. 11, in *The Classics of Western Spirituality*, tr. Colm Luibheid (Mahwah, NJ: Paulist Press, 1985), p. 138.
3. "The Hound of Heaven," *The Poems of Francis Thompson*, ed. Wilfred Meynell (London: Oxford University Press, 1937), pp. 89–94.
4. *The Art of Prayer, op. cit.*, pp. 190–91.
5. Origen, *On Prayer*, in *The Classics of Western Spirituality*, tr. Rowan A. Greer (New York: Paulist Press, 1979); ch. 12, 2; pp. 104–105.
6. St. Basil, *Regulae fusius tractatae*, PG 31, 920C–921B. On this topic of praying always and the doctrine of the Eastern Fathers, see I. Hausherr, S.J., *Hésychasme et Prière* (Rome: Pontifical Oriental Institute, 1966).

7. For a more detailed development of the "Jesus Prayer," see "The Jesus Prayer" in George A. Maloney, S.J., *The Prayer of the Heart* (Notre Dame: Ave Maria Press, 1981), pp. 128–47. Also see I. Hausherr, S.J., *The Name of Jesus*, tr. Charles Cummings, O.C.S.O. (Kalamazoo, MI: Cistercian Publications, Inc., 1978); Cistercian Studies Series, no. 44, "A Monk of the Eastern Church," in *The Prayer of Jesus* (New York: Désclée Co., 1987); *On the Invocation of the Name of Jesus* (Fairacres, Oxford: S.L.C. Press, 1969); Ignatius Brianchaninov, *On the Prayer of Jesus*, tr. Lazarus Moore (London: J. M. Watkins, 1965); Mother Maria, *The Jesus Prayer* (North Yorkshire: The Greek Orthodox Monastery of the Assumption, 1975); Per-Olof Sjorgen, *The Jesus Prayer* (Philadelphia: Fortress Press, 1975).

8. J. Lotz, S.J., *Interior Prayer: The Exercise of Personality* (New York: Herder & Herder, 1965), p. 133.

9. Pseudo-Dionysius, *Mystical Theology*, in *The Soul Afire*, ed. H. A. Reinhold (Garden City, NY: Doubleday, Image Books, 1973), p. 49. This author is called Pseudo-Dionysius because in order to give them greater authority, in his writings he implies that he is the Athenian Dionysius who was converted by St. Paul's preaching in Athens. He probably was a Syrian of the fifth century who was influenced by the writings of St. Gregory of Nyssa.

10. George A. Maloney, S.J., *Prayer of the Heart, op. cit.,* pp. 75–76.

Chapter Nine

1. Rudolf Bultmann, *Theology of the New Testament*, Vol. 2, tr. Kendrick Grobel (New York: Charles Scribner's Sons, 1955), pp. 60–61, 63.

2. Karl Rahner, "Preliminaries," in *Theological Investigations*, Vol. 3, tr. by K.-H. and B. Kruger (London, 1961), pp. 321–22. I highly recommend three doctoral dissertations that deal with this subject of primordial words, and specifically the words "Logos" and "heart" of Christ, which I have found extremely helpful in my research on Rahner's theology of heart: Joseph H. P. Wong, S.D.B., *Logos-Symbol in the Christology of Karl Rahner*, diss. Pontifical Gregorian University (Rome, 1981); Michael J. Walsh: *The Heart of Christ in the Writings of Karl Rahner* (Rome: Gregorian University Press, 1977); Annice Callahan:

Karl Rahner's Spirituality of the Pierced Heart (Lanham, MD: University Press of America, 1985).

3. Cf. Walsh, *op. cit.,* p. 21.

4. "The Theology of the Symbol," *Theological Investigations*, Vol. 4, p. 225.

5. *Theological Investigations*, Vol. 4, p. 252.

6. *Concise Theological Dictionary*, eds. Karl Rahner and H. Vorgrimmler, tr. R. Strachan (New York: Herder and Herder, 1965), p. 203.

7. "Some Theses for a Theology of the Devotion to the Sacred Heart," in *Theological Investigations*, Vol. 3, pp. 331–52. See Walsh, p. 44.

8. Denzinger-Schonmetzer, *Enchiridion Symbolorum, Definitionum et Declarationum*, 34th ed. (Freiburg: Herder, 1965), #300, 318.

9. For a meditative presentation of the attitudes and actions of Christ, the God-man, see Jan G. Bovenmars, M.S.C., *Biblical Spirituality of the Heart* (Staten Island, NY: Alba House, 1991), especially ch. 4, "Jesus' Heart in the New Testament," pp. 78–99.

10. "Theology of the Symbol," in *Theological Investigations*, Vol. 4, tr. K. Smyth (London, 1966), p. 238.

11. It is interesting to note that Rahner's first doctoral dissertation at Innsbruck in 1936 was on the biblical and patristic understanding of the pierced heart of Jesus in John 19:34. *E Latere Christi. Der Ursprung der Kirche als Zweiter Eva aus der Seite Christi des zweiten Adam. Eine Untersuchung über den typologischen Sinn von Jo 19:34*, diss. (Innsbruck, 1936).

12. *The Trinity*, tr. J. Donceel, S.J. (New York: Herder & Herder, 1969), p. 22.

13. *Ibid.*, p. 101.

14. Cf. George A. Maloney, S.J., *Invaded by God: Mysticism and the Indwelling Trinity* (Denville, NJ: Dimension Books, 1979), especially ch. 2, "The Mystery of the Trinity," pp. 43–62.

15. On the Eastern Fathers' teaching on the Trinity as self-giving toward us and all of God's creation through God's uncreated energies, which are primarily the self-giving of each unique person in the Trinity in the unity of their "essential" love, yet with the individuated gift of each person, see George A. Maloney, S.J., *Uncreated Energy* (Warwick, NY: Amity House, 1987).

16. Cf. H. J. Heagney, *"Behold This Heart": The Story of St. Margaret Mary Alacoque* (New York: P. J. Kenedy & Sons, 1947), p. 163.

17. For a discussion of the changing cultural aspects that have accounted for a lack of relevance of the Paray symbols and practices, see John W. Padberg, S.J., *Symbols, Devotions and Jesuits,* in *Studies in the Spirituality of Jesuits,* Vol. 20 (St. Louis, 1988), no. 3, pp. 22–26.

18. Pierre Teilhard de Chardin, *The Divine Milieu,* tr. B. Wall (New York: Harper & Row, 1960), pp. 96–98.

Chapter Ten

1. Dietrich Bonhoeffer, "Thy Kingdom Come, " written in 1932, in D. Godsey, *Preface to Bonhoeffer* (Philadelphia: Fortress Press, 1965), pp. 28–29.

2. E. Schillebeecks, *The Church and Mankind,* in *Concilium* (New York: Paulist Press, 1964), pp. 81–82.

3. The Chalcedonian formulation reads in part: "one and the same Christ, Son, Lord, only-begotten, made known in two natures without confusion, without change, without division, without separation, the difference of the natures being by no means removed because of the union, but the property of each nature being preserved and coalescing in one *prosopon* (person) and *hypostasis,* not parted or divided into two *prosopa,* but one and the same Son, only-begotten, divine Word, the Lord Jesus Christ." See J. N. D. Kelly, *Early Christian Doctrine* (New York: Harper, 1960), p. 340.

4. Amos N. Wilder, "Art and Theological Meaning," in *The New Orpheus: Essays Toward a Christian Poetic,* ed. Nathan A. Scott, (New York: Sheed & Ward, 1964), p. 407.

5. I have treated this patristic vision at length in two works: *The Cosmic Christ from Paul to Teilhard* (New York: Sheed & Ward, 1968) and *Man—The Divine Icon* (Pecos, NM: Dove Publications, 1973).

6. Callahan, *op. cit.,* p. 124ff.

7. Karl Rahner, "Theology and Anthropology," in *Theological Investigations,* Vol. 9, tr. G. Harris (London, 1972), p. 28.

8. Karl Rahner, *Foundations of Christian Faith: An Introduction to the Idea of Christianity,* tr. William V. Dych, S.J. (New York: Seabury-Crossroad Books, 1978), pp. 44–89.

9. Karl Rahner, "Reflections on the Unity of the Love of Neighbor and the Love of God," in *Theological Investigations*, Vol. 6, tr. K.-H. and B. Kruger (London, 1969), p. 247.

10. See Joe McCown, *Availability: Gabriel Marcel and the Phenomenology of Human Openness* (Missoula, MT: Scholars Press, 1978), pp. 79–82.

11. Cited by Christopher F. Mooney, *Teilhard de Chardin and the Mystery of Christ* (New York: Doubleday and Co., Inc., 1966), p. 33

12. *The Future of Man*, tr. N. Denny (New York: Harper, 1964), pp. 82–89.

13. See George A. Maloney, S.J., *The Cosmic Christ from Paul to Teilhard*, pp. 182–220; Robert Hale, O.S.B. Cam.: *Christ and the Universe. Teilhard de Chardin and the Cosmos* (Chicago: Franciscan Herald Press, 1973).

14. *The Phenomenon of Man*, tr. Bernard Wall (New York: Harper Torchbooks, 1959), p. 298.

15. *Super-Humanité, Super-Christ, Super-Charité*, in *Oeuvres de Pierre De Chardin*, Vol. 9 (Paris: Seuil, 1965), pp. 212–16.

16. *Ibid.*, p. 213.

17. *Comment je vois*, unpublished ms.

18. Cited by Maria Gratia Martin, I.H.M., *The Spirituality of Teilhard* (Westminster, MD: Newman Press, 1967), pp. 97–98.